**At Issue**

# Mob Rule or the Wisdom of the Crowd?

# Other Books in the At Issue Series

Athlete Activism
Celebrities in Politics
Male Privilege
The Opioid Crisis
Public Outrage and Protest
Sexual Consent
Student Debt
Universal Health Care
Vaccination
Vaping
Wrongful Conviction and Exoneration

## At Issue

# Mob Rule or the Wisdom of the Crowd?

**Lita Sorensen, Book Editor**

## GREENHAVEN PUBLISHING

Published in 2020 by Greenhaven Publishing, LLC
353 3rd Avenue, Suite 255, New York, NY 10010

Copyright © 2020 by Greenhaven Publishing, LLC

First Edition

All rights reserved. No part of this book may be reproduced in any form without permission in writing from the publisher, except by a reviewer.

Articles in Greenhaven Publishing anthologies are often edited for length to meet page requirements. In addition, original titles of these works are changed to clearly present the main thesis and to explicitly indicate the author's opinion. Every effort is made to ensure that Greenhaven Publishing accurately reflects the original intent of the authors. Every effort has been made to trace the owners of the copyrighted material.

Cover image: Jesadaphorn/Shutterstock.com

**Library of Congress Cataloging-in-Publication Data**

Names: Sorensen, Lita, editor.
Title: Mob rule or the wisdom of the crowd? / Lita Sorensen, book editor.
Description: First edition. | New York : Greenhaven Publishing, 2020 | Series: At issue | Includes bibliographical references and index. | Audience: Grades 9–12.
Identifiers: LCCN 2019022600 | ISBN 9781534506381 (library binding) | ISBN 9781534506374 (paperback)
Subjects: LCSH: Group decision making. | Crowdsourcing.
Classification: LCC HM746 .M63 2020 | DDC 658.4/036—dc23
LC record available at https://lccn.loc.gov/2019022600

*Manufactured in the United States of America*

Website: http://greenhavenpublishing.com

# Contents

**Introduction**     7

1. An Overview of the Wisdom of Crowds Phenomenon     11
   *Graham Kendall*

2. Wisdom of Crowds Only Works When Diversity Is Present     15
   *Will Hutton*

3. A View of the Crowd from a Traditional Social Science Perspective     20
   *Floyd Henry Allport*

4. Democracy and the Crowd     28
   *Talal Al-Khatib*

5. Can the People Ever Be Trusted?     35
   *Julie Simon*

6. Stereotype Accuracy Helps with Efficient Decision-Making     40
   *Lee Jussim*

7. Wikipedia Taps into the Wisdom of the Crowd     52
   *Jeffrey A. Tucker*

8. Is Crowdsourcing Misguided Tech Utopianism as Applied to Government?     56
   *Stefaan Verhulst*

9. Human Swarming and Collective Intelligence     62
   *Louis Rosenberg*

10. Will Collective Intelligence Change the Way We Work?     71
    *MIT Sloan School of Management*

11. Witness to an Information Cascade: The Dangers of Herd Mentality     78
    *Claire Potter*

12. 10 Things You Ought to Know About Polls     88
    *Bill Schneider*

| | |
|---|---|
| 13. Introducing the Global Brain: How Ideas Will Spread in 2035<br>*Michael Haupt* | **96** |
| 14. Better Wisdom from Crowds<br>*Peter Dizikes* | **100** |
| 15. When the Wisdom of Crowds Fails<br>*Nick Beim* | **105** |
| 16. Groupthink Can Lead to Bad Decisions and Hinder Innovation<br>*Phil McKinney* | **109** |
| **Organizations to Contact** | **114** |
| **Bibliography** | **119** |
| **Index** | **124** |

# Introduction

An ancient Chinese proverb has it that "Three stupid shoemakers know more than the wisest man."

The statement can be said to be an argument for the idea of democracy itself, where the wisdom of a crowd, or collective society, can quite often be found to be sounder than the knowledgeable decisions of elites. It's also an old idea, spanning as far back in time to Aristotle and is mentioned in his *Politics*. The idea of mob rule, the negative counterpart to the positive wisdom of the collective, has ancient roots as well and was first referenced by Polybius, a Greek historian of the Hellenic period. He defined it as the pathological version of democracy, where legitimate authorities are intimidated or silenced by a mob or a "fickle crowd." In the Hebrew Talmud, mentions of the Greek word "ochlos," referring to mobs or crowds of any kind as pertaining to the rule of law, abound.

It is truly an old dichotomy, as old as conceptions of human law, philosophy, and even decision making. And yet the ideas are as prescient today as they have ever been. With the rise of modern and increasingly more open and democratic societies and the invention of the internet, a resurgence of interest in these two dichotomous ways of thinking has been pushed to the forefront.

## The Wisdom of the Crowd

In defining the idea of the wisdom of the crowd, the term *crowd* may take on more than the originally-thought of definition of a crowd. One characterization describes a crowd as a group of people actively being asked to participate in a decision-making process. In modern contexts, crowds are often used in online (internet) applications, but they are also used in real life, or offline, capacities. Sometimes, members of a certain crowd may be paid for their participation, such as in paid surveys or polls. Other times, such as in jury duty in the United States, the wisdom of the crowd is mandated or required and not an individual's personal choice.

The wisdom of the crowd is found in the fact that the aggregate of any large group's answers to any given question involving general knowledge, the estimation of quantities, or spatial reasoning is most often found to be superior or at least as good as that of individuals singled out within the group. This phenomenon may be explained by the cancelation of idiosyncratic noise (certain specifics in the outlook of an individual) associated with each judgment. Thus, taking the average over a large number of responses will go some way toward balancing or accommodating the effect of this noise, creating a superior judgment.

## Mob Rule

The term *mob rule* has many more connotations associated with governance and social psychology, where it is sometimes synonymous with crowd psychology. Mob rule has a pejorative context. Social psychologists have many developed theories explaining how crowd psychology and behavior differs from that of individuals, and more theories for the way individuals act within a crowd and ways in which they interact with it. Prominent social scientists who have delved into such theories include such people as Gustave Le Bon, a Frenchman best known for his *The Crowd: A Study of the Popular Mind*, written in 1895; Gabriel Tarde, a French sociologist; Steve Reicher, a present-day British professor prominent in the field of social identity; as well as Sigmund Freud.

Most studies relate to the behaviors and thought processes of both the single members of crowds and the crowd as an entity. It's been shown that crowd behavior is related to individual loss of responsibility and the mistaken impression of a universality of behavior, both increasing with larger crowd sizes.

*At Issue: Mob Rule or Wisdom of the Crowd* encompasses differing viewpoint and contextual articles regarding the idea of mob rule and/or the wisdom of crowds. You will find selections outlining the wisdom of the crowd and wise crowds as theories, introducing author James Surowiecki's influential 2004 book, *The Wisdom of Crowds*, and providing some historical context for consideration. Also included is a serious look at crowd psychology or mob rule as originally conceptualized by social scientists, which perhaps stands in critical analysis of the wisdom of crowds, a piece examining what the United States Founding Fathers felt as far as our fledgling democracy and the wisdom of crowds versus the idea of mob rule, and pieces elucidating how diversity, pluralism, and a truly free press are the ultimate expression of the wisdom of crowds.

In addition, we include pieces on adjunct inventions and phenomenon stemming from the study of crowd behavior and the wisdom of crowds. Crowdsourcing seeks to harness the wisdom of crowds to source goods and services and sometimes ideas and finances (crowdfunding) from a large group of participants usually connected by the internet. As a function, it divides the work between individuals to achieve a cumulative result.

Human swarming, or decentralized, self-organizing networks of individuals acting in real time to solve problems is examined, as is the occurrence of information cascades, when the wisdom of the crowd goes terribly wrong and incites herd-like behavior, leading to poor and blatantly wrong, sometimes dangerous choices. Wikipedia, the free online encyclopedia, which is openly crowdsourced, is introduced as a product of the wisdom of crowds with authors who praise it as well as those who openly criticize it. The Global Brain, a futuristic and neuroscience-inspired vision of a worldwide information and communications technology network that interconnects all people and their technological artifacts is explored, as well as an upgrade to the wisdom of crowds algorithm called Surprisingly Popular.

The concepts of mob rule or the wisdom of crowds are old ideas that have seen increasing relevance today with the advent of the internet, a new technology which has made collaboration and communication more viable than ever before. It is up to human society to decide whether the construction is more of a continuum or two separate dichotomous views competing and to use that knowledge to our best advantage. To that end, a greater understanding of the wisdom of crowds phenomenon and crowd dynamics itself is needed. The viewpoints that make up *At Issue: Mob Rule or the Wisdom of the Crowd* will begin to offer that needed perspective.

# 1

# An Overview of the Wisdom of Crowds Phenomenon

*Graham Kendall*

*Graham Kendall is Professor of Operations Research and Vice-Provost at the University of Nottingham in the United Kingdom. He is the editor-in-chief of the IEEE Transactions of Computational Intelligence and AI in Games, as well as an associate editor of nine other professional journals. Prior to becoming a professor, he worked in the Computer Science industry for almost 20 years.*

*The following is a general introduction to the ideas behind the phenomenon of the wisdom of crowds. In his article for The Conversation, an independent and nonprofit online magazine with a global outreach first launched in Australia in 2011, Kendall cites several examples of how the judgment of crowds usually proves to be correct, and how the diversity and talent of individuals plays a part in predicting the success of crowd decision making. Kendall introduces James Surowiecki's 2004 landmark book, The Wisdom of Crowds, and makes special note of how "Wise Crowds" and independence of thought are necessary for the success of the model.*

The great Victorian polymath, Sir Francis Galton, was at a country fair in 1906, so the story goes, and came across a competition where you had to guess the weight of an ox. Once the

---

"How to Unleash the Wisdom of Crowds" by Graham Kendall, The Conversation, February 10, 2016. https://theconversation.com/how-to-unleash-the-wisdom-of-crowds-52774. Licensed under CC BY-ND 4.0.

competition was over Galton, an explorer, meteorologist, scientist and statistician, took the 787 guesses and calculated the average, which came to 1,197 pounds. The actual weight of the ox was 1,198 pounds. In effect, the crowd had provided a near perfect answer. Galton would later publish this insight in *Nature*.

This phenomenon, where collective wisdom is better than most, if not all of the individuals in the crowd has become known as the Wisdom of Crowds. The authoritative take on it came from James Surowiecki. A more up-to-date example is the "Ask the Audience" part of *Who Wants to be a Millionaire*, where the studio audience are polled and the most popular answer is the correct answer 91% of the time.

Even if there is a better individual guess, you face the problem of deciding which individual's guess to select. If you choose the crowd's guess, the decision is made for you and there is every opportunity that you will get a good answer, certainly better than choosing randomly from the other guesses. The technique has practical uses beyond the quiz show.

## Understanding the *Challenger* Disaster

On January 28, 1986 the space shuttle *Challenger* broke up 73 seconds after launch, killing all seven astronauts on board. The disaster has been well reported in the intervening 30 years, but one intriguing aspect of it may have passed you by.

Almost immediately after the explosion, investors started selling stocks of the four main contractors involved in the Challenger launch—Lockheed, Rockwell International, Martin Marietta and Morton Thiokol. Of the four companies Morton Thiokol fell the most, almost 12% by the end of trading on that day, compared to about 3% for the other three companies.

This was a sign that the stock market felt that Morton Thiokol was to blame for the disaster but without having any firm evidence to hand.

In any case, six months later, the market was proven to be right. The O-ring seals on the booster rockets made by Thiokol were the cause of the problem. Richard Feynman, the renowned physicist, famously presented his findings to the Rogers Commission showing how the seals had failed.

It is still not quite clear how the wisdom of crowds managed to identify the company that was to blame for the disaster within minutes of it happening. Markets always weigh up a variety of factors and it's hard to unpick the rationales at play. It's just about possible that a few investors caught wind of whispers from before the launch about engineers' concerns.

## Finding the *Scorpion* Submarine

On May 22 1968 the US navy lost one of its submarines and wanted to find the wreckage, but the intelligence it had was not able to provide an area that was small enough to effectively search. John Craven, a naval officer, decided to harness the wisdom of crowds.

He asked a wide group of individuals, drawn from diverse backgrounds ranging from mathematicians to salvage experts to guess the submarine's location. The group's average guess was just 220 yards from the location where the *Scorpion* was eventually found.

## What Makes It Work?

The wisdom of crowds might seem like an easy way to to get answers. Simply ask a lot of people [what] they think, and aggregate the answers. If the method could find the *Scorpion* submarine, then a missing plane should be just as easy? Well, no.

As yet, nobody has been able to find the Malaysia Airlines plane MH370 that went missing in March 2014. Almost two years on and the crash site—assuming it crashed—has not been found. That's despite a massive crowdsourcing effort to identify the location of the aircraft, which was detailed in an article on The Conversation. But this was a case of searching for pieces of debris, not making educated guesses about location. And it leads us in to the key rules to follow if you want to use the wisdom of crowds to your advantage.

Four criteria are important in making this an effective tool.

1. **Independence:** The various guesses have to be independent of one another. That is, each person must guess without the knowledge of what other people have guessed.
2. **Diversity:** It is important to have a diverse set of guesses. In the guess the weight of the ox example, the people making the guesses ranged from farmers, butchers, livestock experts, housewives etc. That is, some people would be considered experts, while others would be considered as people with just a passing interest.
3. **Decentralisation:** The people making the guesses should be able to draw on their private, local knowledge.
4. **Aggregation:** There must be some way of aggregating the guesses into a single collective guess. In the guess the weight of the ox example, this was done by taking the average guess. This is a common method, but others may also be used.

Philip Ball, in this BBC article (http://www.bbc.com/future/story/20140708-when-crowd-wisdom-goes-wrong), highlighted flaws in the theory when studies ignore the rules. Remove independence and people start to gravitate towards a consensus which veers away from the accurate answer. Reduce diversity and respondents rely on shared biases, like a room full of football fans predicting results while burdened with the knowledge of which teams are the favourites. In other words, it helps to deploy a bit of wisdom when choosing your crowd.

# 2

## Wisdom of Crowds Only Works When Diversity Is Present

### *Will Hutton*

*Will Hutton is a British political economist, academic administrator, and journalist. He is currently Principal of Hertford College, University of Oxford, and Chair of the Big Innovation Centre, an initiative from the Work Foundation. He was formerly editor-in-chief for* The Observer.

*The wisdom of crowds theory works when individuals come to their own decisions independently as best they can before acting as a group. This is particularly true when morals and values are implicit in the decision. However, irrational following of the herd without much thought can result in mob mentality. The crowd's judgment is best when it includes a variety of individuals with quite different outlooks. When a few people hold the same types of views, decisions can be bad, even harmful, such as with stock market bubbles and government agency misjudgments. Harnessing the wisdom of aggregated views, rather than relying on "intelligence," has more chance of success.*

On Tuesday lunchtime, the English cricket team, triumphant winner of the Ashes, paraded in an open-top, double-decker bus from St Paul's to Trafalgar Square. Beforehand, I must confess I had my doubts. Trafalgar Square celebrations are for great national occasions, I had thought. Winning a Test series against Australia,

"The Crowd Knows Best," by Will Hutton, Guardian News and Media Ltd, September 18, 2005. Reprinted by permission.

although profoundly satisfying, was not on the same scale as winning the World Cup in football or rugby, or even the Olympic bid. It risked, I thought, descending into unjustified jingoism and triumphalism, undermining cricket's tradition of sportsmanship and respect for opponents.

I needn't have worried. Trafalgar Square was much less full and the event shorter than it had been to celebrate England's rugby success. Unlike then, the traffic flowed freely and pedestrians used the wide southern pavement to go about their business as if not much was happening. Although there was pride, it was much more gentle and less hubristic than I expected. In fact, the crowd calibrated the scale and tone of the response perfectly. The celebration turned out to be the right thing to do in the right way.

The crowd had been just as intelligent at the Oval. It knew exactly when the match was won and England's score had become too great for Australia to chase in the time available, when it was safe to stop mocking and joshing the Australian fielders and start congratulating worthy adversaries. Hours before victory had been formally sealed, the magnificent Shane Warne stopped being told he was the man who had dropped the Ashes (Kevin Pietersen would have been out had Warne held the catch, and England's eventual total would probably have been eminently beatable) and was told by thousands of voices rather that they wished he was English. The crowd had decided to become collectively generous, reflecting an aggregated instinct to do the right thing at exactly the right time that it largely managed throughout.

This latter ability of a crowd to home in on a crucial detail—the point at which England was safe—is grist to the mill of James Surowiecki, author of the subtle and intriguing *The Wisdom of Crowds*, one of the most important books of the last year. In his view, one of humanity's greatest assets is our unrecognised ability to get collective decisions right in crowds as long as we each make our individual decision as far as possible independently and are not too much influenced by wanting to follow experts or second-guessing others.

It is when we follow the crowd that it turns into an irrational mob, creating stock market bubbles or lynching the innocent. But when crowd decisions emerge of our own aggregated free will, they are astonishingly accurate and, when values are involved, decent.

Surowiecki starts his book with an exercise in ox-weighing mounted by English scientist Francis Galton in a west of England animal fair in the early 1900s: 787 breeders, sightseers, farmers and labourers were asked to guess the weight of an ox after it had been slaughtered and dressed, with most of the respondents largely ignorant of anything to do with cattle. No individual got the weight right, but the average guess of the crowd was 1,197 lbs. The actual weight turned out, to Galton's amazement, to be 1,198 lbs. The crowd, like that at the Oval and in Trafalgar Square, had shown an extraordinary collective judgment.

*The Wisdom of Crowds* is studded with similar examples and experiments, from audience advice to contestants on *Who Wants to be a Millionaire*? to asking students to guess the temperature of their classroom to finding a way through a maze. In every case, the crowd's decision turns out not only to be right, but consistently better than any individual's. Surowiecki cites the example an American naval commander used to find a sunken submarine lost at sea. After aggregating a mass of guesses of where it might be and then averaging them, he went on to search the location that the crowd thought the submarine would be. It was right to within some 200 yards and miles better than any individual guess.

To be wise, though, the crowd's judgment has to include everyone's—the expert, the stupid, the allegedly commonsensical, the wild, the analytic, the hunch. It's by comprehending the universe of possible outcomes in all their diversity and then averaging them that the wisdom emerges.

Trouble starts, as Surowiecki readily concedes, when individuals start to adjust their first thoughts and reactions with what they think others are thinking, or when judgments are too little influenced by the diverse views of others. Stock market bubbles, classic exercises in collective irrationality, happen because, as [John Maynard] Keynes famously argued, the art of successful stock market investment is to second-guess what the mass of other investors think, so causing prices irrationally to inflate.

And most governmental cock-ups, like [Tony] Blair deluding himself, parliament and the country that Saddam Hussein had weapons of mass destruction, are because a few people holding the same views dominate the decision-making process. One of the lessons of *The Wisdom of Crowds* is that privately generated government "intelligence" by agencies like the CIA or MI6 has a bias to make mistakes because of the narrowness and lack of diversity of the views that they build upon to make their judgments. To assess the time and place of the next terrorist attack, the Met and the Home Office would be best advised to harness the wisdom of aggregated views, thinks Surowiecki, rather than rely on so-called intelligence.

An independent, diverse and inquiring press is also fundamental to collective wisdom. Last week, the crowd nearly made a collective mistake—panic-buying petrol, so generating a self-fulfilling shortage, because of the threatened blockade of petrol refineries. In fact, the blockade was always a bluff without anything like the necessary support. This was something that could have been quickly discovered had the (mainly right-of-centre) newspapers that splashed with the story cared to do some elementary journalism. But that would have spoiled what proved an imaginary story. In fact, the crowd was wiser than the journalism, collectively guessing at the lack of the support, a view quickly validated by a diversity of sources ranging from the BBC to the internet. Petrol mainly ran out (and then only temporarily) in those towns where right-wing newspaper readership dominated, but not in those with more diverse newspaper sales and readerships.

Surowiecki's *Wisdom of Crowds* is thus very contingent. Get closer and the wisdom only manifests itself when there are lots of diverse opinions, plenty of independent sources of information and masses of sturdy individuals reaching their conclusions unaffected by emotionally following the opinion of others. Trying to create the circumstances in which those conditions systematically hold is nigh impossible. But it's nice to know that if and when they do, the average of our aggregated judgments turns out to be right so often. There's no better case for pluralism, diversity and democracy, along with a genuinely independent press. We have to continue aiming for such a world, even if it never arrives.

# 3

## A View of the Crowd from a Traditional Social Science Perspective

### *Floyd Henry Allport*

*Floyd Henry Allport was an American psychologist born in Milwaukee, Wisconsin, in 1890. He is considered the father of experimental social psychology, as he had a preeminent role in the creation of social psychology as a legitimate branch of study. His classic book,* Social Psychology *(1924), has impacted all writings in the field to this day.*

*In this excerpted selection, Floyd Henry Allport essentially offers a criticism of the idea of the wisdom of the crowd. He argues that there is no such thing as crowd behavior and that an attempt to explain social phenomena with this language is misleading—as the true explanation as to behavior is always rooted in the component parts of any group—within each individual's mindset.*

There is no such thing as a group mind; it is a misleading and harmful conception in every way, whether it is applied to crowd behavior, social conflict, revolutions, or the theory of the superorganic: such is the thesis of the author of this pamphlet.

The theory that a crowd possesses a mental life resulting purely from aggregation and superadded to the mental processes of its members seems to have perished at the hands of progress in social science. Its ghost, however, has been exceedingly difficult to lay:

---

"The Group Fallacy in Relation to Social Science," by Floyd Henry Allport, American Psychological Association. Reprinted by permission.

## A View of the Crowd from a Traditional Social Science Perspective

The convenient and picturesque manner of speaking in terms of groups as wholes has infiltrated much of our social thinking. The subtlety of this influence may be partly explained as follows. When we read that a certain army captured a city, or a certain football team defeated a rival team, the language, though not precise, is not misunderstood. It is clear that it is solely the individual soldiers or players who combined their efforts and accomplished the feat described. When we read, however, that the crowd becomes violent, emotional, or intolerant, or that it thinks in images or lacks reason, we are in danger of being misled into thinking that it is a crowd mind rather than the minds of individuals which is accountable for these phenomena. So long as the language is intended and accepted as purely descriptive and metaphorical no confusion exists. But the transition from description to explanation is in such cases very subtle, and not always recognized. The intangibility of the phenomena combines with the collective or abstract use of language to produce an error. This error is the attempt to explain social phenomena in terms of the group as a whole, whereas the true explanation is to be found only in its component parts, the individuals. Such an explanation is in itself false. We do not need a super-mind hypothesis to explain mob action, if we but take the trouble to study the individual in the mob and observe how he is responding to the stimuli afforded by the behavior of his fellows. This neglected field of study is being brought to the foreground by a modern social psychology whose data comprise the social behavior of the individual. The crowd mind theory is not only false; it retards in a special manner the discovery of the truth. Pointing toward the whole rather than the parts it withdraws attention from the latter and incites thought in precisely the wrong direction.

The influence of the social mind theory is as widespread as it is subtle. In the various guises it has assumed it has become amazingly protean. We find a counterpart of it in the social organism metaphor of Plato, as well as in the modern varieties evolved by Spencer, Espinas, and Münsterberg. In these alluring metaphors much space is given to developing a large conception which leads us nowhere;

while the true origin of social organization, the psychology of the individual, has been correspondingly neglected. We meet with the collective error again in the social systems of philosophical idealists. Here it plays freely into the hands of a metaphysics of the objective nature of mind. Professor Bosanquet, for example, argues for the existence of a "general will" which gives definition to individual wills.[1] We meet with the fallacy again in theories of government and morals, where it takes the garb of national spirit, and absolution in conceptions of the State, the Law, and the Right. The abstracted social mind is put back again into the individual as the "collective" or "bee-man" of Sageret[2] as well as in the semi-mystical theories of Sidis[3] and Trotters.[4]

A scholarly attempt to put the social mind hypothesis upon a tenable basis has recently been made by Professor McDougall.[5] In his view, which he calls the "Group Mind," the social reality is alleged to exist not in collective consciousness nor behavior, but in an organization or structure of social relationships which can be conceived to exist only in mental terms. A university, for example, is not comprised in its material aspects, nor even in its personnel. It is systematized relation of individuals and traditions, intangible, but real and mental, and carried along independently of particular individuals. Our answer to this is, of course, that, although not dependent upon particular individuals, this organized tradition is dependent upon some individuals. It exists in the attitudes and consciousness of these separate persons, just as it did in Professor McDougall's mind while he was developing the illustration. So far as we know the group mind has no other form of existence than this, namely in individuals; nor could we conceive of it exerting any effect upon the social order except through these agencies.

But perhaps the best way in which to deal with the fallacy under consideration is to expose its inadequacy when put to the test of explanation. Accepting at face value the social psychology of Le Bon, suppose we proceed, equipped with the concepts of crowd intolerance, emotionality, irrationality, and the like, to explain the actual mob phenomena of modern society. We should find that our terms merely describe, they do not explain. We are ascribing the actions of the mob to things which mobs generally do—which is mere tautology. There is at hand no means for explaining the differences in the behavior of different crowds, since all are emotional, irrational, and the like. Why should the excitability of one crowd express itself in whipping non-church-going farmers, that of another crowd in looting grocery stores, and that of still another in lynching negroes? These questions throw into relief the necessity of delving deeper for our notions of cause than terms which describe the crowd as a whole. We must seek our mechanisms of explanation in the individuals of whom the crowd is composed.

We should fare no better if we were to depend upon the group mind theory for notions of cause. The "group mind" in the sense employed by its exponents is a static mind. It is a result, not a cause, of individual behavior. It offers no provision for explaining social change—change, that is, in the group mind itself. One might, for instance, ask how such a change could have been produced in the organized mental life of a group as the recent change from the tradition and practice of an alcoholic era to a régime of prohibition in our own country. For answers to such questions we must turn again to the responses of individuals to changing material and social environments and to the influence of leaders, inventors, and reformers. Such attempts as have been made to explain social movements in group terms have been purely on the descriptive plane. We may cite as an example Spencer's theory of a progressive, diversifying evolution of the social organism. Such metaphors are descriptive rather than revealing. They express; but they do not explain. They are soon passed by in the serious work of seeking causes.

The views which we have thus far examined are examples of what I have chosen to call the "group fallacy." This fallacy may be defined as the error of substituting the group as a whole as a principle of explanation in place of the individuals in the group. The word "group" is here used in the widest sense. Two forms of the fallacy may be distinguished. The first attempts its explanation in terms of psychology, assuming that it is possible to have a "group psychology" as distinct from the psychology of individuals. The second renounces psychology and relies upon some other form of group process for treatment of cause and effect. Both forms abolish the individual; and, it may be added, both therefore abolish the services of psychology as a possible helpmate of sociology.

Turning from explicit collective mind theories the task now lies before us of pointing out a less easily recognized but widely diffused influence of the fallacy under consideration. I shall present three examples from the more dynamic phases of sociological theory, namely social conflict and social change. These illustrations deal respectively with the psychoanalytic interpretation of group conflicts, the mechanism of revolutions, and the cultural approach to social causation.

## The Group Fallacy in Social Conflict

One of the most interesting varieties of the group fallacy is that which translates mental conflict within the individual into terms of dissociation within a hypothetical social mind. Although a number of writers have dealt with this pathological metaphor, its most elaborate development appears in a posthumous work of the late Dr. W. H. R. Rivers. The following points of fundamental resemblance are observed by him between the neurotic person and the abnormal social order. First, the cause of the disorder in each case lies deeper than the outer manifestations or symptoms. Social diagnosis, like the diagnosis of the psychoanalyst, must penetrate into the hidden forces of life. The prognosis, since the derangement is complex, is also uncertain in both cases. The repression of one portion of society by another is said to be closely analogous to repression and dissociation in the individual. In both cases the repressed element remains and causes trouble when the tension becomes too great. Rivers describes two forms of dissociative process. The first is unwitting: the individual merely turns his back upon that which is unpleasant. Just as we tend to let disagreeable experiences pass out of our attention, so one portion of the group (the upper class) preserves its peace of mind by ignoring the existence of poverty, disease, and kindred evils in the other portion. So far the metaphor is obvious. But if the "social mind" in which such dissociation takes place were to be taken literally there would result a ridiculous confusion. Shall we say for example that the upper classes who do the suppressing are conscious, while the lower classes, since they form the material which is banished from the social mind, are therefore unconscious.

Rivers' second type of dissociation is one in which the individual deliberately and wittingly forces painful experiences from his field of consciousness. The group analogy is that the more fortunate and powerful class of society "deliberately represses outward manifestations of the discontent [among the lower class] which social wrongs arouse." Freud himself invites confusion in this field by applying to the individual a term borrowed from social usage, namely, censorship. And at this point Rivers sounds a note of caution against literal interpretation which he himself does not heed. The persistence of the repressed element, he says, is common to both the neurotic individual and the abnormal group. Tensions are thus created breaking forth as hysterical behavior in the individual and catastrophic change in the social organism. Another type of outlet in the individual is furnished by the symbolism of dreams, which are elsewhere shown by Rivers to be analogous to the symbolism employed by the repressed faction of the social order. Thus a primitive tribe subjugated by a more powerful people preserved their religious ceremonies, but gave them a disguised character so as to conceal from the conquerors their true meaning. Hanging a hated person in effigy is another example of the social use of symbolism to release feeling without incurring punishment. The similarity of such mechanisms to the individual dream process is not to be questioned. We have no justification, however, for alleging dissociation and symbolism to be mechanisms of an "over-individual," or a "social mind." We have here a collection of individual inhibitions. A mental conflict exists between struggle responses against the oppressors on the one hand, and avoidance of punishment on the other. It is really a struggle between anger and fear. But this conflict and its release through symbolism lie, so far as the mechanism of explanation is concerned, wholly within the individual. To expand these mechanisms to the proportions of dissociation within a social mind is to destroy their significance.

Parenthetically, we are reminded of a contemporary instance of social conflict and evasion to which the collective viewpoint might be amusingly applied. There is said to be an unwritten law of censorship adhered to by managers of low class theatricals. It is this: that any stage joke, no matter how salacious its meaning, may be allowed to pass if it has also a different meaning intelligible to those who are too pure minded to comprehend the other. This arrangement is indeed convenient, for it permits the clergyman and the roué to sit side by side in the front row, each enjoying the performance from his own angle, while the tranquility of the social mind remains serenely undisturbed!

That the pathological form of the group fallacy leads in precisely the wrong direction is evident upon closer analysis of the relation between social conflict and mental conflict. A significant fact taught us through psychoanalysis is that one horn of the dilemma present in mental conflict is usually social in character. It consists of a system of socialized habits inculcated in the individual through stimulation by others, and striving in opposition to the unmodified egoistic drives. We deny ourselves immediate cravings because to satisfy them would infringe upon the needs and desires of others. Were it not for this denial, an overt or actual conflict would result between ourselves and other members of society. To avoid such social conflict the socialized reactions inhibit the unsocialized, and between them engender in the individual a mental conflict. Sometimes it is fear of the social environment rather than socialized habits which represents the social force in the conflict. Thus in Rivers' example of veiled ceremonials the lower class, not daring to risk overt social combat with their masters, develop in themselves a mental conflict between hate and fear which finds its release in some disguised manner. On the other hand, when the members of the upper class shut out of their consciousness the miseries of the lower, this behavior holds sway only in the absence of overt conflict. When the masses rise in revolt the scene of the conflict is at once shifted from within the mind of the aristocrat to the field of outward combat between groups. At every turn therefore social and mental conflict are inversely related in their occurrence. The more the conflict lies within the individual, the less it lies within the group, and vice versa. Instead therefore of using the mechanism of individual neurosis to explain conflict in terms of the group as a whole, we must conclude that that mechanism is precisely the one which cannot be used in that manner. Mental conflict is surely an important concept for understanding social causation; but the interpretation must always be through a collectivity of individual conflicts, and never as a phenomenon of the group as such.

[…]

## Notes

1. "The Notion of a General Will." MIND, 1920, 77–81.
2. "Remarques sur la psychologie collective." REV. PHIL., 1919, Vol. 87, 465–474.
3. The Source and Aim of Human Progress. Journal of Abnormal Psychology ans Social Psychology, 1919, Vol. 14, 91–143.
4. *Instincts of the Herd in Peace and War.*
5. *The Group Mind.*

# 4

## Democracy and the Crowd
### Talal Al-Khatib

*Talal Al-Khatib is an American author who has written about media, government, and technology. He currently serves as an executive communications adviser for Chevron. He holds a master's degree in communications from John Hopkins University.*

*Writing during the chaotic 2016 election cycle, Al-Khatib examines what the United States Founding Fathers had to say about democracy, which can be seen as one permutation of the wisdom of the crowd. He notes that when it came down to it, most of the signers of the Constitution appeared to have mixed feelings, with some opposing even the use of the word, fearing mob rule. Further, Al-Khatib gives context to the term "socialism" from a historical and international point of view.*

In an election season as chaotic as this one, when less than a third of Americans believe the presidential campaign process is working as it should according to a recent Gallup poll, looking back at how the Founding Fathers envisioned the course of our nation can be a helpful exercise in reasserting our values as a democracy.

But when it comes to the idea of democracy, the Founding Fathers had mixed feelings, with some outright opposing the very use of the word.

"Even Founding Fathers Worried About Democracy," by Talal Al-Khatib, Group Nine Media, April 4, 2016. Reprinted by permission.

"Democracy was an epithet," said Joseph Ellis, author of the Pulitzer-winning book, *Founding Brothers: The Revolutionary Generation*, in a 2012 interview. "Democracy meant mob rule. Democracy meant conceding the issue to people who don't understand it."

Many of the Founding Fathers were instead more apt to describe the nascent government as a republic. The word "democracy" never once appears in the Declaration of Independence of the Constitution.

The Federalist Papers, specifically Federalist No. 10, written by James Madison, who would later become the fourth president of the United States, expounded on the differences between a pure democracy, defined as "a society consisting of a small number of citizens, who assemble and administer the government in person," which only offers no remedy for the "mischiefs of faction," and a democratic republic, which "promises the cure for which we are seeking."

Alexander Hamilton, one of the most influential voices in the interpretation of the US Constitution, was particularly skeptical of a pure democracy. In a speech given on June 21, 1788 at the New York convention to ratify the Constitution, Hamilton explained:

> *It has been observed by an honorable gentleman, that a pure democracy, if it were practicable, would be the most perfect government. Experience has proved, that no position in politics is more false than this. The ancient democracies, in which the people themselves deliberated, never possessed one feature of good government. Their very character was tyranny; their figure deformity: When they assembled, the field of debate presented an ungovernable mob, not only incapable of deliberation, but prepared for every enormity. In these assemblies, the enemies of the people brought forward their plans of ambition systematically. They were opposed by their enemies of another party; and it became a matter of contingency, whether the people subjected themselves to be led blindly by one tyrant or by another.*

If some of the nation's founders like Hamilton found flaws with direct democracy, as practiced in ancient Greece, they almost certainly would have taken issue with a number of features of the modern political landscape, such as ballot measures and presidential primaries.

In fact, many of the nation's fathers opposed the creation of political parties at all. They had seen how wrangling by political interests in Europe affected nations across the Atlantic. In his Farewell Address in 1796, George Washington warned:

> *However [political parties] may now and then answer popular ends, they are likely in the course of time and things, to become potent engines, by which cunning, ambitious, and unprincipled men will be enabled to subvert the power of the people and to usurp for themselves the reins of government, destroying afterwards the very engines which have lifted them to unjust dominion.*

Americans might not have much confidence in the election process—and the Founding Fathers likely wouldn't have liked it much either.

At a speech in Georgetown University last week, Democratic presidential candidate Bernie Sanders of Vermont, who identifies as a "Democratic socialist," gave a defense of the ideology long maligned and often misunderstood in US history. Invoking the legacies of Presidents Franklin D. Roosevelt and Lyndon B. Johnson, Sanders summed up his political philosophy as rebalancing a system of government that promotes economic inequality in favor of the middle class. Sanders detailed how his ideology informs the positions he takes on domestic issues, including minimum wage, tax policy, college tuition and more. Embracing the socialist label is a gambit for any candidate, given that it is a term historically used as a political epithet. How has America's relationship with socialism evolved over our history? And how did socialism acquire such a negative connotation in American politics?

Americans often associate socialism with European governments, particularly in Scandinavia. And in fact, socialism arrived in the United States in the 19th century as a European import, brought over by German immigrants. The earliest traces of socialism in the United States can be found in small communes, such as Brook Farm or New Harmony, the intended design of which is seen here, set up as radical social experiments. At the time, the United States was rapidly industrializing, drawing people to urban centers for work, often for low wages and in oppressive conditions. These communities offered an alternative to the social stratification common in American cities. Unfortunately for the members of these early utopian or religious socialist communes, they often found themselves rattled by financial difficulties, leadership squabbles or feuds between factions that would lead to their dissolution within a matter of years of their founding.

Socialism within the United States first received national attention following the publication of a science fiction book by Edward Bellamy called *Looking Backward*, published in 1888. The book depicts the United States as a socialist utopia in the year 2000, in which industry has been nationalized and goods are equally distributed among workers. It would go on to become the third-largest bestseller of the late 19th-century, behind *Uncle Tom's Cabin* and *Ben-Hur: A Tale of the Christ*, and spark what were known as "Bellamy clubs" to discuss the political and economic themes explored in the book. Naturally, a book as successful as *Looking Backward* led to sequels, satires and sharply critical responses.

Largely influenced by the political philosophy of Karl Marx, German immigrants arriving on American shores formed small political parties or trade unions based on socialist principles. These groups advocated for social justice, labor reforms and more. Founded in 1901, the Socialist Party of America, the product of a merger between the Socialist Labor Party and the Social Democratic Party, promoted "democratic socialism." Unlike state socialism, in which the means of production are owned by the government, democratic socialism advocates for industry under worker control. Democratic socialists also differ from Communists, who promote revolutionary socialism through militant action, and instead seek political reform through elections, which is also why democratic socialists are typically advocates of universal suffrage. The socialist movement benefited from close alliances with the labor movement, and the two were closely intertwined. This often meant that the occasionally violent tactics used in labor strikes reflected poorly on socialists due to guilt by association.

In 1912, the socialists could count more than 100,000 party members on its rolls. At the time, Eugene V. Debs was the movement's figurehead, drawn to the movement following his involvement in a labor strike. He was a political leader with strong labor connections who would run for president five times. Debs didn't succeed in his run for the presidency in 1912, but other candidates on the socialist ticket did, including 160 councilmen, 56 mayors and even a congressman.

In 1910, Wisconsin voters sent to the House of Representatives the first Socialist ever elected to Congress, Victor L. Berger. Born in 1860 in Austria-Hungary, Berger immigrated to the United States at 18 years old, settling in Milwaukee, becoming a teacher and later newspaper publisher. Upon reaching Congress, Berger's most notable act was authorizing a constitutional amendment to abolish the US Senate. After serving in the 62nd Congress, Berger lost reelection, but returned to run again, regaining his seat in 1918, before losing it again, and regaining it once more to serve three additional terms. Berger retained his seat even as socialists were falling out of favor in national politics.

Just as the socialist movement was finding its footing in the American electoral landscape, it made a major strategic error in opposing US involvement in World War I. While this position helped boost its fortunes in 1911, it proved near fatal to the group once the war was underway. In response to the Russian revolution, which saw the deaths of millions of people and the overthrow of the government, US legislators passed the Espionage Act of 1917, which urged patriotism and made it a crime to speak out against US wartime actions or the draft. The penalties for violating the act could be one or two decades in jail. Prior to the act's passage, socialists often held anti-war demonstrations and encouraged draft dodging. As soon as the act passed, thousands were targeted for arrest, including Debs, who received a 10-year sentence and was stripped of his citizenship. Although Debs would run again for president in 1920 from behind bars and was eventually pardoned, his time in prison took a toll on his health and marked the end of his political career. The combination of government suppression and the Red Scare also led to the collapse of party membership numbers. Norman Thomas … became the new party leader with Debs out of the picture, and the movement's membership increasingly became more middle class and intellectual and less tied to labor.

Although the Great Depression offered the socialists an opportunity at the ballot box, after the trouble they had connecting with the upwardly mobile middle class voter in the roaring 20s, Americans instead voted Franklin D. Roosevelt into office in 1932. Roosevelt swiftly enacted a "New Deal" program aimed at alleviating unemployment and oversaw the passage of pro-labor legislation, efforts that saw Roosevelt branded a socialist by opponents in the business and banking communities. In his book *The Road to Serfdom,* economist Friedrich A. Hayek coins the term "creeping socialism" to define how increased government control over the economy and labor lead to a socialist society. Hayek lamented that this transition toward socialism was unhealthy not only for the economy but the character of the worker. Although Hayek focused on Britain, he specifically referenced the New Deal in his work.

With the end of World War II came the Cold War, a period of political, economic and military tension between East, represented by the Soviet Union and its Communist allies, and West, including the United States and its NATO allies. Fear of Communists lingering within American communities led to the second Red Scare. This would be the era of black lists, nuclear panic and McCarthyism, named after notorious Communist witch-hunter Sen. Joseph McCarthy … By the 1950s, socialist parties in the United States had no more than a couple thousand members, their movement politically untenable in an era of rabid anti-Communism. The nation also experienced an economic boom that made socialism far less appealing to the average middle-class American household.

Since the 1950s, socialist movements have been associated with political extremes in the United States, particularly the far left. But policies inspired by socialist politics still exist today. Social Security, created during the Roosevelt administration, Medicare, set up during the Johnson administration, and other similarly redistributive programs provide government assistance to financially insecure citizens. With the financial crisis and increasing concerns over economic inequality, polls have suggested an increasing tolerance of socialist ideas in the American political dialogue.

According to a recent Gallup poll, nearly half of Americans said they would vote for a socialist candidate for president, though that label tested the worst with voters among other political, religious and demographic considerations for an office-seeker.

# 5

# Can the People Ever Be Trusted?

*Julie Simon*

*Julie Simon is a writer and researcher specializing in policy research. She was the Head of Government Innovation Research in the Policy and Research Team at Nesta and also has worked for the Young Foundation and the Social Market Foundation.*

*Representative democracy hinges on the theory that most people are incapable of making good decisions. That is why we elect leaders to represent us and make those decisions for us. But what if the people are wiser than they're given credit for? What if mass participation is the better way to make good decisions? Crowdsourcing might be the answer to helping governments solve certain problems, though it appears that this isn't a solution for all issues. If public officials can tap into the ways to best capitalize on public engagement, citizens could have more say.*

Democratic theory has tended to take a pretty dim view of people and their ability to make decisions. Many political philosophers believe that people are at best uninformed and at worst, ignorant and incompetent. This view is a common justification for our system of representative democracy—people can't be trusted to make decisions so this responsibility should fall to those who have the expertise, knowledge or intelligence to do so.

"When Is the Crowd Wise or Can the People Ever Be Trusted?" by Julie Simon, Opening Governance, October 2, 2016. http://opening-governance.org/blog/2016/10/2/when-is-the-crowd-wise-or-can-the-people-ever-be-trusted. Licensed under CC BY SA 4.0 International

Think back to what Edmund Burke said on the subject in his speech to the Electors of Bristol in 1774, "Your representative owes you, not his industry only, but his judgement; and he betrays, instead of serving you, if he sacrifices it to your opinion." He reminds us that "government and legislation are matters of reason and judgement, and not of inclination." Others, like the journalist Charles Mackay, whose book on economic bubbles and crashes *Extraordinary Popular Delusions and the Madness of Crowds*, had an even more damning view of the crowd's capacity to exercise either judgement or reason.

The thing is, if you believe that "the crowd" isn't wise then there isn't much point in encouraging participation—these sorts of activities can only ever be tokenistic or a way of legitimising the decisions taken by others. There are then those political philosophers who effectively argue that citizens' incompetence doesn't matter. They argue that the aggregation of views—through voting—eliminates "noise" which enables you to arrive at optimal decisions. The larger the group, the better its decisions will be.

The corollary of this view is that political decision making should involve mass participation and regular referenda—something akin to the Swiss model. Another standpoint is to say that there is wisdom within crowds—it's just that it's domain specific, unevenly distributed and quite hard to transfer. This idea was put forward by Friedrich Hayek in his seminal 1945 essay on *The Use of Knowledge in Society* in which he argues that:

> ... the knowledge of the circumstances of which we must make use never exists in concentrated or integrated form, but solely as the dispersed bits of incomplete and frequently contradictory knowledge which all the separate individuals possess. The economic problem of society is thus not merely a problem of how to allocate 'given' resources ... it is a problem of the utilization of knowledge not given to anyone in its totality.

Hayek argued that it was for this reason that central planning couldn't work since no central planner could ever aggregate all the knowledge distributed across society to make good decisions.

More recently, Eric Von Hippel built on these foundations by introducing the concept of information stickiness; information is "sticky" if it is costly to move from one place to another. One type of information that is frequently "sticky" is information about users' needs and preferences. This helps to account for why manufacturers tend to develop innovations which are incremental—meeting already identified needs—and why so many organisations are engaging users in their innovation processes: if knowledge about needs and tools for developing new solutions can be co-located in the same place (i.e. the user) then the cost of transferring sticky information is eliminated.

These assumptions about the distributed nature of knowledge underpin both concepts of open innovation and collective intelligence. The latter was popularised by James Surowiecki in his book *The Wisdom of Crowds*, in which he argued that crowdsourcing is a superior method for, among other things, sampling and forecasting. Essentially, he describes the phenomenon of aggregating information in groups, where the information it aggregates doesn't have to be perfect and you don't need smart participants to get smart aggregate decisions. The concept of open innovation has similar theoretical foundations and is based on the idea that a single organisation can't contain all the knowledge and skills required to develop new products and services and should source these ideas externally.

If one subscribes to the view that knowledge is widely distributed across society, then the task for policymakers is to tap into this expertise, which then has implications for the kind of engagement that's necessary—it could mean a greater focus on crowdsourcing or collaboration with small groups of expert citizens rather than, for example, mass voting or polling.

There is growing evidence on how crowdsourcing can be used by governments to solve clearly defined technical, scientific or informational problems. Evidently there are significant needs and opportunities for governments to better engage citizens to solve these types of problems. There's also a growing body of evidence on how digital tools can be used to support and promote collective intelligence.

Nesta's recent research on the subject has examined how innovative patient organisations are working as collectives to assemble and analyse information involved in healthcare, and in particular in managing long term conditions. Some of these patient organisations are already supporting the development of peer relationships, driving landmark research programmes, sharing skills and unlocking the energy and expertise of patients. Indeed, our research demonstrates that where citizens are highly motivated regarding specific issues they can and do self-organise to access, interpret and distribute large amounts of complex information and take decisive action in innovative campaigns.

But what about problems which are normative or values based? Can the tools and principles of open innovation be applied to democratic institutions such as parliaments and political parties which are arenas for contestation about the public good, and not simply marketplaces for ideas?

For example, experts can tell you how to build a nuclear power station but they can't really tell you whether you should build power stations since that isn't a purely technical question. In these cases, it's not entirely straightforward what a "good decision" might look like. If there is no such thing as an objectively correct answer then why not open it up to the crowd—especially where there is significant public appetite? If you take the Hayekian view, the crowd are more likely to come to an optimal decision than a group of elected representatives.

However, is the aggregation of votes really the best mechanism for getting a smart answer? As our ongoing research suggests, in some cases, it's just as useful to understand the plurality of opinions and relative priorities as it is to understand the majority view. So, for example, if you simply ask people how a city should spend its infrastructure budget you will probably get a list of ideas and lots of comments without really any understanding of people's relative priorities. However, if you structure a participatory budgeting process to enable people to vote and comment on their favourite ideas, and rank their priorities, then public officials will have far greater information on which to make decisions.

For some questions, there are no straightforward yes or no answers. Where the question is particularly complex, it might be as useful to know why people vote in a particular direction, as much as whether they vote yes or no. In some cases, a completely legitimate answer might be "maybe, it depends." One good example of this is the recent referendum on the UK's membership of the EU. Even though a majority of the voting public voted to leave the EU, it's not at all clear why we voted to leave. The yes/no vote didn't give an indication of people's relative priorities in terms of trade, controls on immigration, sovereignty, public spending or the myriad other issues discussed during the campaign. There is currently no consensus on what Brexit means and there is no mandate for one type of Brexit over another since the referendum didn't ask the public what it might want from a new kind of relationship with the EU.

So, the critical task for public officials is to have greater clarity over the purpose of engagement—in order to better understand which methods of engagement should be used and what kinds of groups should be targeted.

At the same time, the central question for researchers is when and how to tap into collective intelligence: what tools and approaches can be used when we're looking at arenas which are often sites of contestation? Should this input be limited to providing information and expertise to be used by public officials or representatives, or should these distributed experts exercise some decision making power too? And when we're dealing with value based judgements when should we rely on large scale voting as a mechanism for making "smarter" decisions and when are deliberative forms of engagement more appropriate? These are all issues we're exploring as part of our ongoing programme of work on democratic innovations.

# 6

# Stereotype Accuracy Helps with Efficient Decision-Making

## Lee Jussim

*Lee Jussim is a social psychologist and former department chair at Rutgers University. He headed up the Scientific Integrity/Best Practices in Science Group at Stanford's Center for Advanced Study in the Behavioral Sciences (2013–2015). His* Social Perception and Social Reality: Why Accuracy Dominates Self-Fulfilling Prophecy and Bias *(Oxford University Press) received the American Publisher's Association award for best book in psychology of 2012. Much of his recent work has focused on how faculty politics and confirmation biases distort social science conclusions.*

*Most of us are taught not to give in to stereotypes, that they are dangerous and potentially harmful. However, this viewpoint turns this notion on its side, noting that if stereotypes are not true then perhaps the "stereotypes" that are true are not stereotypes after all. In fact, in social psychology studies, stereotype accuracy is highly replicable. According to research, when individuating information is clear and relevant, stereotype effects tend to be weak or nonexistent, but when there is little or no such information then people are influenced by stereotypes.*

"Stereotype Accuracy Is One of the Largest and Most Replicable Effects in All of Social Psychology," by Lee Jussim. Reprinted by permission.

Psychological perspectives once defined stereotypes as inaccurate, casting them as rigid (Lippmann, 1922/1991), rationalizations of prejudice (Jost & Banaji, 1994; La Piere, 1936), out of touch with reality (Bargh & Chartrand, 1999), and exaggerations based on small "kernels of truth" (Allport, 1954/1979; Table 1). These common definitions are untenable. Almost any belief about almost any group has been considered a "stereotype" in empirical studies. It is, however, logically impossible for all group beliefs to be inaccurate. This would make it "inaccurate" to believe that two groups differ or that they do not differ.

Alternatively, perhaps stereotypes are only inaccurate group beliefs, and so therefore accurate beliefs are not stereotypes. If this were true, one would first have to empirically establish that the belief is inaccurate—otherwise, it would not be a stereotype. The rarity of such demonstrations would mean that there are few known stereotypes. Increasing recognition of these logical problems has led many modern reviews to abandon "inaccuracy" as a core definitional component of stereotypes (see Jussim et al, 2016 for a review).

Nonetheless, an emphasis on inaccuracy remains, which is broadly inconsistent with empirical research. My book, *Social Perception and Social Reality: Why Accuracy Dominates Bias and Self-Fulfilling Prophecy* (hence SPSR), reviewed 80 years of social psychological scholarship and showed that there was widespread emphasis on inaccuracy. Some social psychologists have argued that the "kernel of truth" notion means social psychology has long recognized stereotype accuracy, but I do not buy it. It creates the impression that, among an almost entirely rotten cob, there is a single decent kernel, the "kernel of truth." And if you doubt that is what this means, consider a turnabout test (Duarte et al, 2015): How would you feel if someone described social psychology has having a "kernel of truth?" Would that be high praise?

## The Empirical Evidence

This blog is not the place to review the overwhelming evidence of stereotype accuracy, though interested readers are directed to SPSR and our updated reviews that have appeared in *Current Directions in Psychological Science* (Jussim et al, 2015) and Todd Nelson's *Handbook of Stereotypes, Prejudice and Discrimination* (Jussim et al, 2016). Summarizing those reviews:

1. Over 50 studies have now been performed assessing the accuracy of demographic, national, political, and other stereotypes.

2. Stereotype accuracy is one of the largest and most replicable effects in all of social psychology. Richard et al (2003) found that fewer than 5% of all effects in social psychology exceeded r's of .50. In contrast, nearly all consensual stereotype accuracy correlations and about half of all personal stereotype accuracy correlations exceed .50.[1]

3. The evidence from both experimental and naturalistic studies indicates that people apply their stereotypes when judging others approximately rationally. When individuating information is absent or ambiguous, stereotypes often influence person perception. When individuating information is clear and relevant, its effects are "massive" (Kunda & Thagard, 1996, yes, that is a direct quote, p. 292), and stereotype effects tend to be weak or nonexistent. This puts the lie to longstanding claims that "stereotypes lead people to ignore individual differences."

4. There are only a handful of studies that have examined whether the situations in which people rely on stereotypes when judging individuals increases or reduces person perception accuracy. Although those studies typically show that doing so increases person perception accuracy, there are too few to reach any general conclusion. Nonetheless, that body of research provides no support

whatsoever for the common presumption that the ways and conditions under which people rely on stereotypes routinely reduces person perception accuracy.

## Bian and Cimpian's "Generic" Critique

[Lin] Bian and [Andrei] Cimpian step into this now large literature and simply declare it to be wrong. They do not review the evidence. They do not suggest the evidence is flawed or misinterpreted. Bian & Cimpian simpl[y] ignore the data. That sounds like a strong charge, but, if you think it is too strong, I request that you re-read their critique. The easiest way to maintain any cherished belief is to just ignore contrary data—something that is distressingly common, not only in social psychology (Jussim et al, in press), but in medicine (Ioannidis, 2005), astronomy (Loeb, 2014), environmental engineering (Kolowich, 2016), and across the social sciences (Pinker, 2002).

How, then, do Bian and Cimpian aspire to reach any conclusion about stereotype accuracy without grappling with the data? Their critique rests primarily on declaring (without empirical evidence) that most stereotypes are "generic" beliefs, which renders them inherently inaccurate, so no empirical evidence of stereotype inaccuracy is even necessary. This is the first failure of this critique. They report no data assessing the prevalence of stereotypes as generic beliefs. An empirical question ("what proportion of people's stereotypes are generic beliefs?") can never be resolved by declaration.

That failing is sufficient to render their analysis irrelevant to understanding the state of the evidence regarding stereotype accuracy. However, it also fails on other grounds, which are instructive to consider because they are symptomatic of a common error made by social psychologists. They fall victim to the processistic fallacy, which was addressed in SPSR. Thus, my response to these critiques begins by quoting that text (p. 394):

*To address accuracy, research must somehow assess how well people's stereotypes (or the perceptions of individuals) correspond*

> with reality. The evidence that social psychologists typically review when emphasizing stereotype inaccuracy does not do this. Instead, that evidence typically demonstrates some sort of cognitive process, which is then presumed—without testing for accuracy—to lead to inaccuracy ...

Social psychologists have many "basic phenomena" that are presumed (without evidence) to cause inaccuracy: categorization supposedly exaggerates real differences between groups, ingroup biases, illusory correlations, automatic activation of stereotypes, the ultimate attribution error, and many more. None, however, have ever been linked to the actual (in)accuracy of lay people's stereotypes. Mistaking processes speculatively claimed to cause stereotype inaccuracy, for evidence of actual stereotype inaccuracy, is the prototypical example of the processistic fallacy.

Their prototypical cases of supposedly inherently erroneous generic beliefs are those such as "mosquitos carry the West Nile virus" and "ducks lay eggs" (Leslie, Khemlani, & Glucksberg, 2011). They cite evidence that people judge such statements to be true. They argue that this renders people inaccurate because few mosquitos carry West Nile virus and not all ducks lay eggs. Ipso facto, according to their argument, stereotypes that are generic beliefs also cannot be accurate.

Even if people's beliefs about ducks' egg laying were generic and wrong, we would still have no direct information about the accuracy of their beliefs about other people. So, how does this translate to stereotypes? Bian and Cimpian cite another paper by [Sarah-Jane] Leslie (in press) in support of the claim that "more people hold the generic belief that Muslims are terrorists than hold the generic belief that Muslims are female." What was Leslie's (in press) "evidence"? Quotes from headline-seeking politicians and a rise in hate crimes post-9/11. In short, this is no evidence whatsoever that bears on the claim that "more people believe Muslims are terrorists than Muslims are female." Of course, even if this were valid, how it would bear on stereotype accuracy is entirely unclear, because that would depend, not on researcher assumptions about what people mean when they agree with statements like, "Muslims are terrorists" but on evidence assessing what people actually mean. The stereotyping literature is so strongly riddled with invalid researcher presumptions about lay people's beliefs, that, absent hard empirical evidence about what people actually believe, researcher assumptions that are not backed up by evidence do not warrant credibility.

If, as seems to be widely assumed in discussions such as Bian and Cimpian's, agreeing that "Muslims are terrorists" means "all Muslims are terrorists" then such stereotypes are clearly inaccurate (indeed, SPSR specifically points out that all or nearly all absolute stereotypes of the form ALL of THEM are X are inherently inaccurate, because human variability is typically sufficient to invalidate almost any such absolutist claim). However, the problem here is the presumption that agreeing that "Muslims are terrorists" is equivalent to the belief that "all Muslims are terrorists." Maybe it is, but if so, that cannot be empirically supported just because researchers say so. I suspect many would agree that "Alaska is cold" (indeed, I would myself)—but doing so does not necessarily also entail the assumption that every day in every location in Alaska is always frigidly cold. Juneau routinely hits the 70 degree mark, which I do not consider particularly cold. Yet, I would still agree that "Alaska is cold." Whether any particular generic beliefs is, in fact, absolutist requires evidence. In the absence of such evidence, researchers are welcome to present their predictions as speculations about stereotypes' supposed absolute or inaccurate content, but they should not be presenting their own presumptions as facts.

Bian and Cimpian acknowledge that statistical beliefs are far more capable of being accurate, but then go on to claim that most stereotypes are not statistical beliefs, or, at least, generically based stereotypes are more potent influences on social perceptions. They present no assessment, however, of the relative frequencies with which people's beliefs about groups are generic versus statistical. Again, there is an assumption without evidence.

But let's consider the implications of their claim that most people's stereotypes include little or no statistical understanding of the distributions of characteristics among groups. According to this view, laypeople would have little idea about racial/ethnic differences in high school or college graduate rates, or about the nonverbal skill differences between men and women, and are clueless about differences in the policy positions held by Democrats and Republicans. That leads to a very simple prediction—that people's judgments of these distributions would be almost entirely unrelated to the actual distributions; correlations of stereotypes with criteria would be near zero and discrepancy scores would be high. One cannot have it both ways. If people are statistically clueless, then their beliefs should be unrelated to statistical distributions of characteristics among groups. If people's beliefs do show strong relations to statistical realities, then they are not statistically clueless.

We already know that the predictions generated from the "most stereotypes are generic and are therefore statistically clueless" are disconfirmed by the data summarized in SPSR, and in Jussim et al (2015, 2016). Bian and Cimpian have developed compelling descriptions of the processes that they believe should lead people to be inaccurate. In point of empirical fact, however, people have mostly been found to be fairly accurate. Disconfirmation of such predictions can occur for any of several reasons:

1. The processes identified as "causing" inaccuracy do not occur with the frequency that those offering them assume (maybe most stereotypes are not generic).
2. The processes are quite common and do cause inaccuracy, but are mitigated by other countervailing processes that increase accuracy (e.g., perhaps people often adjust their beliefs in response to corrective information).
3. The processes are common, but, in real life, lead to much higher levels of accuracy than those emphasizing inaccuracy presume (see SPSR for more details).
Regardless, making declarations about levels of stereotype

inaccuracy on the basis of a speculative prediction that some process causes stereotype inaccuracy, rather than on the basis of evidence that directly bears on accuracy, is a classic demonstration of the processistic fallacy.

## The Black Hole at the Bottom of Most Declarations that "Stereotypes Are Inaccurate"

In science, the convention is to support empirical claims with evidence, typically via a citation. This should be an obvious point, but far too often, scientific articles have declared stereotypes to be inaccurate either without a single citation, or by citing an article that itself provides no empirical evidence of stereotype inaccuracy. My collaborators and I (e.g., Jussim et al, 2016) have taken to referring to this as "the black hole at the bottom of declarations of stereotype inaccuracy." For example:

> … *stereotypes are maladaptive forms of categories because their content does not correspond to what is going on in the environment (Bargh & Chartrand, 1999, p. 467).*

There is no citation here. It is a declaration without any provided empirical support.

Or consider this:

> *The term* stereotype *refers to those interpersonal beliefs and expectancies that are both widely shared and generally invalid (Ashmore & Del Boca, 1981). (Miller & Turnbull, 1986, p. 233).*

There is a citation here—to Ashmore and Del Boca (1981). Although Ashmore and Del Boca (1981) did review how prior researchers defined stereotypes, they did not review or provide empirical evidence that addressed the accuracy of stereotypes. Thus, the Miller and Turnbull (1986) quote also ends in an empirical black hole. Bian and Cimpian's argument that "stereotypes are inaccurate" based on studies that did not assess stereotype accuracy is a modern and sophisticated version of this argument from a black hole.

## Is Your Belief in Stereotype Inaccuracy Falsifiable?

That question is directed to all readers of this blog entry who still maintain the claim that "stereotypes are inaccurate." Scientific beliefs should at least be capable of falsification and correction; otherwise, they are more like religion.

Bian and Cimpian follow a long and venerable social psychological tradition of declaring stereotypes inaccurate without: 1. Grappling with the overwhelming evidence of stereotype accuracy; and 2. Without providing new evidence that directly assesses accuracy. This raises the question, *if 50 high quality studies demonstrating stereotype accuracy across many groups, many beliefs, many labs, and many decades is not enough to get you to change your mind, what could?*

I can tell you what could change my belief that the evidence shows most stereotypes are usually at least fairly accurate. If most of the next 50 studies on the topic provide little or no evidence of inaccuracy, I would change my view. Indeed, in our most recent reviews (Jussim et al, 2015, 2016) we pointed out two areas in which the weight of the evidence shows inaccuracy. National character stereotypes are often inaccurate when compared against Big Five Personality measures (interestingly, however, they are often more accurate when other criterion measures are used); and political stereotypes (e.g., people's beliefs about Democrats versus Republicans, or liberals versus conservatives) generally exaggerate real differences. Show me the data, and I will change my view.

If no data could lead you to change your position, then your position is not scientific. It is completely appropriate for people's morals to inform or even determine their political attitudes and policy positions. What is not appropriate, however, is for that to be the case, and then to pretend that one's position is based on science.

## Bottom Lines

Stereotype accuracy is one of the largest effects in all of social psychology. Given social psychology's current crisis of replicability, and widespread concerns about questionable research practices (e.g., Open Science Collaboration, 2015; Simmons et al, 2011), one might expect that social psychologists would be shouting to the world that we have actually found a valid, independently replicable, powerful phenomena.

But if one did think that, one could not possibly be more wrong. Testaments to the inaccuracy of stereotypes still dominate textbooks and broad reviews of the stereotyping literature that appear in scholarly books. The new generation of scholars is still being brought up to believe that "stereotypes are inaccurate," a claim many will undoubtedly take for granted as true, and then promote in their own scholarship. Sometimes, these manifest as definitions of stereotypes as inaccurate; and even when stereotypes are not defined as inaccurate, they manifest as declarations that stereotypes are inaccurate, exaggerated, or overgeneralized. Social psychologists are unbelievably terrific at coming up with reasons why stereotypes "should" be inaccurate, typically presented as statements that they "are" inaccurate. Social psychologists are, however, often less good at correcting their cherished beliefs in the face of contrary data than many of us would have hoped (Jussim et al, in press).

Self-correction is, supposedly, one of the hallmarks of true sciences. Failure to self-correct in the face of overwhelming data is, to me, a threat to the scientific integrity of our field. Perhaps, therefore, most of us can agree that, with respect to the longstanding claim that "stereotypes are inaccurate," a little scientific self-correction is long overdue.

## References

Allport, G. W. (1954/1979). *The Nature of Prejudice* (2nd edition). Cambridge, MA : Perseus Books.

Ashmore, R. D., & F. K. Del Boca (1981). "Conceptual Approaches to Stereotypes and Stereotyping." In D. L. Hamilton (ed.), *Cognitive Processes in Stereotyping and Intergroup Behavior* (pp.1-35). Hillsdale, NJ: Erlbaum.

Bargh, J. A., & T. L. Chartrand (1999). "The Unbearable Automaticity of Being." *American Psychologist*, 54, 462-479.

Duarte, J. L., J. T. Crawford, C. Stern, J. Haidt, L. Jussim, & P. E. Tetlock (2015). Political Diversity Will Improve Social Psychological Science." *Behavioral and Brain Sciences*, 38, 1-54.

Ioannidis, J. P. (2012). "Why Science Is Not Necessarily Self-Correcting." *Perspectives on Psychological Science*, 7, 645-654.

Jost, J. T., & M. R. Banaji (1994). "The Role of Stereotyping in System-Justification and the Production of False Consciousness." *British Journal of Social Psychology*, 33, 1-27.

Jussim, L. (2012). *Social Perception and Social Reality: Why Accuracy Dominates Bias and Self-Fulfilling Prophecy*. New York: Oxford University Press.

Jussim, L., T. Cain, J. Crawford, K. Harber, & F. Cohen (2009). "The Unbearable Accuracy of Stereotypes." In T. Nelson (ed.), *Handbook of Prejudice, Stereotyping, and Discrimination* (pp.199-227). Hillsdale, NJ: Erlbaum.

Jussim, L., J. T. Crawford, & R. S. Rubinstein (2015). "Stereotype (In)accuracy in Perceptions of Groups and Individuals." *Current Directions in Psychological Science*, 24, 490-497.

Jussim, L., J. T. Crawford, S. M. Anglin, J. R. Chambers, S. T. Stevens, & F. Cohen (2016). "Stereotype Accuracy: One of the Largest and Most Replicable Effects in All of Social Psychology." In T. Nelson (ed.), *Handbook of Prejudice, Stereotyping, and Discrimination* (second edition; pp. 31-63). New York: Psychology Press.

Jussim, L., J. T. Crawford, S. M. Anglin, S. M. Stevens, & J. L. Duarte. (In press). "Interpretations and Methods: Towards a More Effectively Self-Correcting Social Psychology." *Journal of Experimental Social Psychology*.

Kolowich. S. (February 2, 2016). "The Water Next Time: Professor Who Helped Expose Crisis in Flint Says Public Science Is Broken." *Chronicle of Higher Education*. Retrieved on 2/3/16 from: http://chronicle.com/article/The-Water-Next-Time-Professor/235136/.

Kunda, Z., & P. Thagard (1996). "Forming Impressions from Stereotypes, Traits, and Behaviors: A Parallel-Constraint-Satisfaction Theory." *Psychological Review*, 103, 284-308.

LaPiere, R. T. (1936). "Type-Rationalizations of Group Antipathy." *Social Forces*, 15, 232-237.

Leslie, S. J. (in press). "The Original Sin of Cognition: Fear, Prejudice and Generalization." *The Journal of Philosophy*.

Leslie, S., S. Khemlani, & S. Glucksberg (2011). Do All Ducks Lay Eggs? The Generic Overgeneralization Effect. *Journal of Memory and Language*, 65, 15–31.

Lippmann, W. (1922/1991). *Public Opinion*. New Brunswick, NJ: Transaction Publishers.

Loeb, A. (2014). "Benefits of Diversity." *Nature: Physics*, 10, 616-617.

Miller, D. T., & W. Turnbull (1986). "Expectancies and Interpersonal Processes." *Annual Review of Psychology*, 37, 233-256.

Open Science Collaboration. (2015). "Estimating the Reproducibility of Psychological Science." *Science*, 349, aac4716. doi: 10.1126/science.aac4716

Pinker, S. (2002). *The Blank Slate*. New York City: Penguin Books.

Richard, F. D., C. F. Bond Jr., & J. J. Stokes-Zoota (2003). "One Hundred Years of Social Psychology Quantitatively Described." *Review of General Psychology*, 7, 331-363.

Simmons, J. P., L. D. Nelson, & U. Simonsohn (2011). "False-Positive Psychology Undisclosed Flexibility in Data Collection and Analysis Allows Presenting Anything as Significant." *Psychological Science*, 22, 1359-1366.

# Endnotes

1. Consensual stereotypes refer to beliefs shared by a group and are usually assessed by means. For example, you might be teaching a psychology of 30 students and ask them to estimate the college graduation rates for five demographic groups. Consensual stereotype accuracy can be assessed by correlating the class mean on these estimates with, e.g., Census data on graduate rates for the different groups. Personal stereotype accuracy is assessed identically, but for each person, separately. So, one would assess Fred's personal stereotype accuracy by correlating Fred's estimates for each group with the Census data. See SPSR, Chapter 16, for a much more detailed description of different aspects of stereotype accuracy and how they can be assessed.

# 7

## Wikipedia Taps into the Wisdom of the Crowd
*Jeffrey A. Tucker*

*Jeffrey Tucker is a former Director of Content for the Foundation for Economic Education. He is the Editorial Director at the American Institute for Economic Research, a managing partner of Vellum Capital, the founder of Liberty.me, Distinguished Honorary Member of Mises Brazil, economics adviser to FreeSociety.com, research fellow at the Acton Institute, policy adviser of the Heartland Institute, founder of the CryptoCurrency Conference, member of the editorial board of the Molinari Review, an adviser to the blockchain application builder Factom, and author of five books.*

*In the internet age, crowdsourcing allows organizations to tap into the wisdom of the crowd through new technology. It can offer suggestions about the selection of the right crowd and how organizations may select an appropriate activity for crowdsourcing, whether it be through competition or collaboration. There is perhaps no better example of crowdsourcing than Wikipedia, an online resource that taps into the wisdom of the collective rather than the mind of a single elite mind. Wikipedia has changed the rules about obtaining knowledge in this digital and crowdsourcing age.*

In the 6th century, Saint Isidore of Seville set out to write a book containing all human knowledge. That's quite an ambition! The

---

"Wikipedia Is the Wonder of the World that Wasn't Supposed to Work," Jeffrey A. Tucker, Foundation for Economic Education, March 10, 2017. https://fee.org/articles/wikipedia-is-the-wonder-of-the-world-that-wasn-t-supposed-to-work/. Licensed under CC BY 4.0 International.

result was astonishing: 20 volumes with 448 chapters with the title *Etymologiae*.

And talk about longevity. The book was a "bestseller" for 1,000 years. To put this in context, this would be like you turning to a book written in 1017 to find out what's what. Let's just say some information would be missing.

The expertise of one person was fine, but now we can crowdsource and collaborate, creating a new form of expertise.

After the printing press, the task of writing encyclopedias became easy, but the method remained the same: a leading expert would dispense knowledge to everyone else.

Wikipedia was founded January 15, 2001, a beautifully symbolic date—a new millennium!—to signal the new way we discover, cumulate, and iterate information flows in the digital age.

The expertise of one person was fine, so long as this was all that our tools permitted. But now we can crowdsource and collaborate. This creates a new form of expertise, a new kind of global knowledge base, one that extracts diffuse information from manifold sources into a single shared portal that can be universally distributed. And more importantly: mistakes can be corrected. Forever. And ever. This is in essence of an adaptive complex system. There is no end state. There is endless progress.

As of this writing, Wikipedia has 27 billion words in 40 million articles in 293 languages. Did I mention that it is free? Yes, this does disemploy the once-famous door-to-door encyclopedia salesmen.

## Proof of Concept

We love and adore Wikipedia, the world over. We also know that it is not the final source or authority. It is a starting place for our research. When known errors are discovered, they are fixed. You've got a problem with an entry? Take the initiative and fix it. It is not perfect, but every discovery of imperfection is an opportunity for change. This is the way, one day at a time, one edit at a time, that Wikipedia has become a wonder of the world.

It was not always so. For the first ten years, the platform was ridiculed, put down, denounced, sneered at, dismissed. Then one day we awoke and realized: wait, this thing has become amazing. (Wikipedia has a nice entry on the critics through the years.)

Wikipedia is the realization of Hayek's solution to the localized knowledge problem.

The founder of Wikipedia is Jimmy Wales. He is the featured speaker at FEEcon, June 15–17, 2017, in Atlanta, Georgia. FEE is deeply honored to have him. His innovation has changed the world.

The insight that made Wikipedia possible is not an accident. Wales was a student of F. A. Hayek's work, in particular, "The Use of Knowledge in Society." Hayek explained the impossibility of centralizing reliable, true, operational knowledge. He explained that this is why markets work. They rely on the localized, specialized, and carefully calibrated knowledge—it's the best we have—of the endpoints in the system. Acting and choosing, people draw on knowledge that is decentralized and diffuse. The knowledge that makes what we call society possible is not given unto a single mind, whether an intellectual or a planning agent. It is inarticulate and even inaccessible to everyone but the actor. Wikipedia took this source of power within markets and built a platform that created a market for knowledge. As Wales explains it, the old way of gathering reliable information was to gather it from the outside in, and then the expert sorted through what is valuable and became the distribution source. The new way gives opportunities for anyone who knows anything to contribute to building.

## Where Are the Rules?

The very first impulse for any critic was to say: this can never work because there are no rules. But remember the first rule of adaptive systems: problems elicit answers. The result has been an evolving set of norms. You might think of this as a market for law. Unlike state law, it is adaptive to change, rooted in humility, and elicits compliance through willing acquiescence. It is something we choose.

The contrast with old-world encyclopedias is striking. The editor would assign a leading expert to write an entry to reflect the consensus of the experts. The results were frozen until the next edition came out. There was vast slippage since nothing could be challenged or changed. The latest scholarship made no difference. They were wonderful for what they were but now we have something better.

FEE would love to invite St. Isidor as a speaker. Unfortunately, that is not really possible. But he is now the patron saint of the Internet.

Jimmy Wales is a great substitute.

# 8

## Is Crowdsourcing Misguided Tech Utopianism as Applied to Government?
*Stefaan Verhulst*

*Stefaan Verhulst is the Co-Founder and Chief Research and Development Officer of the Governance Laboratory at New York University GovLab and is currently responsible for building a research foundation on how to transform governance utilizing science and technology. He is the author or editor of many publications with a focus on new technology and society, including the book,* Self Regulation and the Internet, *published in 2004 and co-authored by Monroe Price.*

*In this overview of current thinking regarding the use of crowdsourcing to enhance modern governance, Verhulst offers criticism of the tendency to see internet applications as end-all answers to difficult or complex questions, citing problems associated with the idea of the wisdom of the crowd that exists offline. He also discusses specific and unique ways crowdsourcing is used in the public sphere that differ from the usual concept of mass wisdom.*

In response to the widespread utopianism regarding the ability of crowdsourcing to provide solutions to difficult problems in both the public and private spheres, Maggie Koerth-Baker warns in this week's *New York Times Magazine* that treating crowds, real

---

"The Wisdom of Crowds in Opening Government" by Stefaan Verhulst, The Governance Lab, December 22, 2012. http://thegovlab.org/the-wisdom-of-crowds-in-opening-government/. Licensed under CC BY-SA 4.0.

or virtual, like sentient beings is misguided. With Wikipedia's success and inescapability playing a large role, Koerth-Baker notes that, "over the last decade, we've come to think of virtual crowds as sources of wisdom that can't be found in individuals." Similarly, in the non-digital world, crowds are often treated as singular entities that, if mishandled or left to their own devices, are prone to irrationality and panic. Beyond questions of how technological mediation could possibly shift the character of a crowd from one defined by thoughtlessness and irresponsibility to one of intelligence and innovation, the underlying conceit, that crowds are entities, rather than groups of individual people, is "deeply flawed."

Koerth-Baker believes that this misconception at least partially derives from the belief that a crowd behaves like a herd of animals, and that, "at some point, it reaches a critical mass and the will of the crowd overrides individual intelligence and individual decision making." In reality, a crowd can be smart or dumb, helpful or dangerous, but, "a crowd's behavior depends on what individuals are thinking and how they interact with one another—not some overpowering collective consciousness."

While Koerth-Baker does not discount the unprecedented collaborative capabilities created by new information technologies, she highlights the importance of not only the individuals within groups, but the information that is being shared by groups, which, necessarily, determines the direction of any collaboration. Essentially, Koerth-Baker argues, while many put faith in crowdsourcing exclusively based on faith in technologically mediated crowds, what really matters for the success or failure of a given collaborative project depends on three things:

- who makes up the crowd,
- the information they share and
- how they interact.

Based on Koerth-Baker's article, it would be easy to question the ability of crowdsourcing in the government arena to address the problems that inspired their creation. However, in an article about the many types of crowdsourcing in government and their potential, Justine Brown helps demonstrate why painting all public sector crowdsourcing projects with the same brush would be reductive.

In the article, Brown lists five central types of crowdsourcing in government: crowd competition, crowd collaboration, crowd voting, crowd funding and crowd labor. This list shows that not all types of crowdsourcing depend on some elusive mass knowledge. For some open government projects, engaging the crowd is done to widen the search for individuals with innovative ideas or insights. A crowd competition, for example, does not place excess faith in the abilities of an undefined crowd entity; rather, it provides incentive and opportunity for an individual or small group of individuals to solve a problem that has eluded more traditional government problem solvers.

The government website Challenge.gov provides a number of crowd competition opportunities for citizens. Challenges like "Non-invasive Measurement of Intra-cranial Pressure" from the National Aeronautics and Space Administration demonstrate that government crowdsourcing projects are often initiated in the hopes of finding a uniquely capable individual, not in the interest of obtaining insight from the crowd as a whole.

US Chief Technology Officer Todd Park, whose Health Datapalooza is one of the more well-known examples of crowd competitions, highlights why they are effective tools for governments: "I think [prizes and competitions] are a very exciting new tool that government has in its toolkit to get better results at a lower cost. You can greatly broaden and deepen the range of players that can help solve the problem. You draw in unusual suspects along with the more usual suspects."

Crowd labor also does not rely on any innate ability or intelligence in the crowd that does not exist in individuals. Instead, it, again, widens the net, but this time instead of doing so in an attempt to find a uniquely capable or insightful individual, the government engages the crowd in the hopes that a large enough group of people will be willing to take up a tedious task so that the task's completion is not left to paid government employees. One such example comes from the Library of Congress, where they are asking the crowd to aid in tagging photos with metadata. While there is no reason to believe that an online crowd is uniquely capable of handling the task, in comparison to paid employees or a real life mass of people, and there is every opportunity for unreasonable individuals within the crowd to attempt to sabotage the project by providing incorrect information, engaging a willing mass of people to undertake necessary but tedious projects within government helps to move more projects to completion while minimizing the time and resources expended by the government itself.

Crowd voting programs, on the other hand, do rely on the masses exhibiting some type of intelligence and reason, but, at some point, even if the outcomes could prove dubious, public opinion must be drawn upon as part of a functional democracy. Similarly, crowd collaboration requires some amount of faith in the crowd, but, for the most part, the reason why many believe that these programs will have success has less to do with an unreasonable faith in crowds than with the hope that the destruction of "sectorial boundaries" will allow previously separated but similarly capable individuals from different areas of interest to work together and engage problems in new and innovative ways.

Some recent high profile examples of crowdsourcing within governments have come from Europe, and, for the most part, they do not fall into the trap that Koerth-Baker warns against. In Estonia, in response to high-profile cases of government corruption, citizens were called upon to provide policy suggestions to be debated on by government officials and possibly implemented. In Iceland, citizen input from Facebook and Twitter was used to help guide officials in crafting a new constitution for Europe's most sparsely populated state. The final document was put together by a 25-member Constitutional Council that drew upon citizens' social media input. Finally, in Finland, any policy petition that obtains 50,000 citizen signatures automatically elicits a vote by the Eduskunta, the Finnish Parliament. Similar programs also exist in the UK and US, but the UK initiative requires 100,000 signatures for Parliament to consider debating the issue, and the US We the People site guarantees only that the administration will "review" and "respond to" petitions that gain at least 25,000 signatures in one month.

Each of the above programs mitigates the power of the people by ensuring that crowdsourcing only serves to set the agenda for the traditional powers that exist within government. While some might argue that this serves to entrench the status quo and traditional power dynamics, it also keeps the government from placing excessive faith in the capabilities of a singular crowd, as Koerth-Baker warns against, and ensures that public funds will not be utilized in the construction of a Death Star. Moreover, while many point to Wikipedia as the ultimate example of the wisdom of the unorganized crowd, it is actually the product of a similar system. Though much of the original content on Wikipedia comes from tens of thousands of outsiders, "the bulk of the changes to the original text … are made by a core group" of around 1400 heavy editors that make thousands of small changes to increase the accuracy of postings. In other words, the masses are relied upon to do much of the grunt work, just as in government crowd labor projects, and to increase the visibility of relevant topics, but a smaller, more trusted group is responsible for shaping the input of the crowd into the final—though, of course, constantly evolving—product.

The German Pirate Party's Liquid Feedback system, on the other hand, essentially sets the party's platform through crowdsourcing. One of the party's defining characteristics is its sliding scale of direct and representative democracy. In this system, party members can vote on any and every issue, if they so choose, or they can delegate their vote on any given issue to their elected representative. On the Liquid Feedback system, proposals are revised and voted upon, and, no matter the opinions of elected representatives, proposals accepted by the crowd become the party's platform. This is certainly the purest example of direct democracy out of the recent crowdsourcing programs, but it also puts the most faith in the wisdom of a singular crowd.

Faith in the transformative power of crowdsourcing in government is not limited to the developed world, however. In parts of Africa, where mobile networks have bypassed all other forms of infrastructure development in terms of speed and usage, "crowdsourcing is increasingly viewed as a core mechanism of new systemic approaches to governance addressing the highly complex, global, and dynamic challenges of climate change, poverty, armed conflict, and other crises." Whether or not the crowdsourcing programs put into place to address these crises correctly characterize what a crowd is and what it is not, of course, remains to be seen.

# 9

## Human Swarming and Collective Intelligence
*Louis Rosenberg*

*Louis Rosenberg is the CEO of the artificial intelligence company Unanimous AI. He is a noted technologist and inventor whose company became famous in 2016 when its swarm intelligence technology correctly predicted the results of the Academy Awards, the Kentucky Derby, the Super Bowl, and the rise of Donald Trump. Rosenberg received his BA, MA, and PhD degrees at Stanford University.*

*In the following viewpoint, Louis Rosenberg introduces the concept of human swarming. According to the author, human swarming is when cohesive groups of individuals work together as unified dynamic systems to create collective intelligence. This is distinguishable from crowds, which may be discordant. The author relates how human swarms differ from simple crowdsourcing by fostering collaboration through the use of synchronous real time online tools enabling a group to move toward collective intelligence and eventually, artificial intelligence (AI). Rosenberg predicts human swarming will have great value in the years to come and provides a ray of hope for anyone who worries about a bleak future where humans feel disconnected from one another.*

"Human Swarming and the Future of Collective Intelligence," by Louis Rosenberg, Singularity Weblog, July 20, 2015. Reprinted by permission.

## Human Swarming and Collective Intelligence

It all goes back to the birds and the bees. The fish too. Even slime-molds. Really, it goes to all social creatures that amplify their collective intelligence by forming real-time synchronous systems. We have many names for these natural assemblages, including flocks, schools, shoals, blooms, colonies, herds, and swarms. Whatever we call them, one thing is clear—millions of years of evolution produced these highly coordinated behaviors because of the survival benefits they provide to a great many species. In this way, nature had demonstrated that social creatures, by functioning together in closed-loop systems, can outperform the vast majority of individual members when solving problems and making decisions, thereby boosting overall survival of their population.[1,2]

For convenience I use the word "swarm" to refer to cohesive groupings of individual members, all working together as a unified dynamic system, their collective behavior tightly coordinated by real-time feedback loops. Unlike discordant groups (i.e. crowds), swarms behave as unique entities, operating as a coherent unit that displays emergent intelligence, even emergent personality. With that definition in mind, the big question that has propelled my explorations over the last few years is simply this: "Can humans swarm?"

Certainly humans didn't evolve the ability to swarm, for we lack the innate connections that other species use to establish feedback-loops among individual members. Ants use chemical traces. Fish detect vibrations in the water around them. Bees use high speed gestures. Birds detect motions propagating through the flock. Whatever method is used for establishing the interstitial connectivity, the resulting swarms possess capabilities as a group that the individuals alone can't match. For example, high speed feedback-control among flapping birds enables thousands of starlings to make precision hairpin turns in winds gusting to 40 miles per hour. It's simply remarkable.

But what about humans? We don't possess the natural ability to form real-time swarms, but can we design technologies that fill in the missing pieces, using artificial means to form the critical interstitial connections? And if so, will swarming allow us humans to achieve the same types of intelligence amplification that other species have attained via synchrony? If we consider the leap in intelligence between an individual ant and a full ant colony working as one, can we expect the same level of amplification as we go from single individual humans to an elevated "hyper-mind" that emerges from real-time human swarming?

I founded Unanimous AI with these questions in mind. Now 18 months into platform development, I feel confident in answering a few of the basics. Yes, humans can swarm. And yes, new technology is the key. Humans can swarm only if we develop technologies that fill in the missing pieces evolution hasn't yet provided. More specifically, swarming can occur among groups of online users by "closing the loop" around populations of networked individuals such that they behave as a real-time synchronous system. This is what we've been working on at Unanimous and the results are very exciting.

I should point out, I'm not talking about simple "crowd sourcing" that employs votes or polls or markets to sequentially aggregate input from large numbers of individuals. Those methods have great value when it comes to characterizing populations, but they don't allow a population to express itself as a coherent unified entity. Polls and votes and markets reveal the average sentiments within groups, identifying central trends, but that's not the same thing as allowing a group to think as one, the parties negotiating in real-time until the group converges on solutions that optimizes support and satisfaction.

The fact is, polls are polarizing, highlighting the differences in populations without doing anything to help groups find common ground. Swarms on the other hand, are unifying, enabling groups to find the commonality among them and converge on solutions that optimize support. Said another way, polls promote entrenchment, driving groups apart, while swarms foster collaboration, pulling groups together. And it's the "together"

## Human Swarming and Collective Intelligence

aspect of swarms that enables a group to unleash its emergent, collective intelligence.

This is why I believe online tools for groups need a major overhaul, moving away asynchronous polling and voting, to synchronous real-time systems—human swarms that can attack a problem together. I know this sounds like a jump in technical complexity, and it is, but it is also a return to our roots. After all, millions of years of evolution suggest that swarms are better suited for unleashing group intelligence.

Consider the humble Slime Mold—It's a single celled organism that congregates by the millions to form a super-cell that behaves as a single unified entity. And although each individual cell is very simple, the unified swarm can successfully forage woodlands for rotting vegetation. In fact, slime molds have been shown by researchers at Hokkaido University in Japan to be able to navigate mazes, finding the shortest and most efficient route between two points of food.[3,4] In other words, as a unified swarm these very simple cells display collective intelligence that exceeded any of the individuals. This brings us back to people. Can we see similar benefits?

This question was purely theoretical until last year when we started testing UNU™, our real-time platform for human swarming. As an online environment that closes the loop around networked users, UNU is the computational glue that allows people to work together in swarms that can answer questions, make decisions, generate ideas, even express opinions. And thus far, the results have been fascinating, suggesting that enhanced intelligence through human swarming is a very real possibility.

When using the UNU platform, swarms of online users can answer questions and make decisions by collaboratively moving a graphical puck to select from a set of possible answers. The puck is generated by a central server and modeled as a real-world physical system with a defined mass, damping and friction. Each participant in the swarm connects to the server and is provided a controllable graphical magnet that allows the user to freely apply force vectors on the puck in real time. The puck moves in response to swarm's influence, not based on the input of any individual participant, but based on a dynamic feedback loop that is closed around all swarm members. In this way, real-time synchronous control is enabled across a swarm of distributed networked users.

Through the collaborative control of the graphical puck, a real-time physical negotiation emerges among the networked members. This occurs because all of the participating users are able to push and pull on the puck at the same time, collectively exploring the decision-space and converging upon the most agreeable answers. But do the answers have value?

To test the value of human swarms, researchers at Unanimous A.I. enlisted groups of novice users and asked them [to] perform a number [of] verifiable intellectual tasks. For example, these groups were asked to make predictions about the winners of the NFL playoffs, the Golden Globes, the Super Bowl, the 2015 Oscars, the Stanley Cup, the NBA finals, and most recently the Women's World Cup. In all cases, the predictions made by swarms were more accurate than the predictions made by the individuals who comprised the swarms. In fact, the swarms consistently performed better than even the most skilled individuals in each group. The swarm also exceeded the tally of "votes" given by the groups, trumping the traditional methods of characterizing populations. In short, initial testing suggests that human swarms do more than reveal the "wisdom of the crowd"—they can unlock the collective intelligence of populations.

For example, when predicting the 2015 Academy Awards, we asked 48 individuals to predict the top 15 award categories. Using the most popular predictions to represent "the wisdom of the crowd," the group collectively achieved 6 correct predictions for the top 15 award categories (40% success). This was our baseline dataset, the low success rate reflecting the fact that this group of users had no special knowledge about movies. To test swarming, we then selected a sub-group of the full population and asked them to make the same predictions, but now as a unified swarm. The sub-group were typical performers on the written poll, ensuring equity. Never-the-less, when working as a unified swarm, the group achieved 11 correct predictions for the top 15 award categories (73% success). We believe this is a very promising result and speaks to the potential for harnessing the wisdom of social groups through real-time swarming.

Just like biological swarms, these artificial swarms have the capacity to outperform the individuals who comprise it. And that makes good sense, for the benefits of swarming are as natural as, well … the birds and bees. Even more exciting is that swarm intelligence offers humanity a way to build enhanced intelligences without replacing ourselves with bits and bytes. In fact, I view human swarming as a safer form of A.I., for it uses technology to produce emergent intelligence, but does so while keeping people in the loop, ensuring that human sensibilities and moralities are integral to its thought processes.

In fact, I see human swarming as the first "human-in the loop" approach to A.I., for it combines the benefits of computational infrastructure and software efficiencies, with the unique values that humans bring to the table in terms of creativity, empathy, morality, and justice. And because a swarm-based emergent intelligence is rooted in human input, the resulting intelligence, no matter how smart, is highly likely to be aligned with humanity not just in values and morals, but goals and objectives. We can't say that about a pure A.I., which could easily have goals and objectives that are not aligned at all with our own. And because we can't prevent researchers from creating pure A.I. technologies that may rival humanity, it's my hope that human swarming will offer us a way to stay one step ahead of the machines. After all, we have billions of brains, and with tools like UNU to connect us in swarms, we may one day be able to boost our intellectual abilities as a society.

Of course, we must ask another question—will people want to swarm? After all, just because swarming provides intellectual benefits, that doesn't mean that large numbers of people will want to collaborate in swarms to answer questions and make decisions. It was with this uncertainty in mind that we interviewed a great many users to capture their subjective feedback after engaging in real-time swarming experiences.

It turns out, most people who try swarming agree—swarms are fun. In a study performed recently at California State University with college seniors, 60% rated the experience of swarming as "very fun" on a subjective scale, with no users expressing negative feelings. Of course, we have to ask ourselves a fundamental question—why? What is it about working together in swarms that triggers the feeling of "fun" in users?

Again, it all goes back to evolution—at least, that's my best guess. When users come together in swarms, they're engaging in a synchronous activity that makes them feel connected to others in real-time. They become part of something larger than themselves.

This affinity for synchrony has deep roots in human development and has been cited as the reason people are inherently drawn to music and dance, as well as team sports. A recent study at UCLA showed even just having groups march together in rhythm gives participants a greater sense of cohesion, group confidence, and enhanced capacity for coordination. This isn't surprising. Many studies have shown that coordinated activities enhance cooperation and allegiance within groups.[5,6,7,8,9]

Synchrony gives people an emotional and physiological rush whether they're jamming in a band or executing a double-play. Similar effects are seen across the animal kingdom, especially in social animals like primates and whales, which use synchronous group behavior as shows of strength, solidarity, and cohesion.[10,11,12] And now, with swarming platforms like UNU, the benefits of real-time synchrony are brought into online social environments, connecting people all over the world for collaborative experiences that are naturally satisfying, unifying, and fun.

So if swarming is both productive and fun, users will flock to systems that enable it. Human swarming will transition from an intellectual curiosity to a powerful tool that unleashes group intelligence in a wide variety of fields, applications, and settings.

Fortunately, the swarms are growing quickly. Just last week, the largest real-time swarm was formed by 88 eager users, all working in unison to answer dozens of questions.

Overall, I am more excited than ever about the promise of human swarming. I see tools like UNU bringing people together in fun new ways, while in the process boosting human intelligence to new levels. Looking to the future, I see swarming as offering great value on many fronts, from enabling truly social forms of social media where content is not just shared by groups but created by groups working together as an emergent intelligence, to providing humanity a more human-friendly alternative to traditional A.I, for swarming builds new intelligences while keeping humans in the loop. It all goes back to the old saying, many minds are better than one. I believe this is true, especially if by pooling our intellectual resources, we humans can stay one step ahead of pure A.I. alternatives.

## Notes

1. Deneubourg, J. L., and S. Goss. "Collective Patterns and Decision Making." *Ethology, Ecology, & Evolution* 1: 295-311, 1989.
2. Axelrod R., and W. D. Hamilton. "The Evolution of Cooperation." *Science* 211:1390–1396, 1981.
3. http://www.scientificamerican.com/article/brainless-slime-molds/.
4. http://www.itsokaytobesmart.com/post/37228609143/beyond-their-pretty-remarkable-ability-to-think.
5. McNeill, W. H. *Keeping Together in Time: Dance and Drill in Human History.* Harvard University Press: 1995.
6. Hagen, E. H., and G. A. Bryant. "Music and Dance as a Coalition Signaling System." *Human Nature*, 14, 21-41, 2003.
7. Marsh, K. L., M. J. Richardson, and R. C. Schmidt. "Social Connection Through Joint Action and Interpersonal Coordination." *Topics Cog Sci.* 1, 320-339, 2009
8. Wiltermuth, S. S., and C. Heath. "Synchrony and Cooperation." *Psychol. Sci.* 20, 1-5, 2009.
9. Reddish P., J. Bulbulia, and R. Fischer. "Does Synchrony Promote General Pro-Sociality?" *Relig, Brain & Behav.* 4, 3-19, 2013.

*Mob Rule or the Wisdom of the Crowd?*

10. Cusick J.A,, and D. L. Herzing. "The Dynamics of Aggression: How Individual and Group Factors Affect the Long-Term Interspecific Aggression Between Two Sympatric Species of Dolphin." *Ethology.* 120 287–303, 2014.
11. Senigalia, V, R. de Stephanis, P. Verborgh, and D. Lusseau. "The Role of Synchronized Swimming as Affiliative and Anti-Predatory Behavior in Long-Finned Pilot Whales." *Behav. Processes.* 91, 8–14, 2012.
12. Fedurek P., Z. P. Machanda, A. M. Schel, and K. E. Slocombe. "Pan Hoot Chorusing and Social Bonds in Male Chimpanzees." *Anim. Behav.* 86, 129–196, 2013.

# 10

# Will Collective Intelligence Change the Way We Work?

## MIT Sloan School of Management

*The MIT Sloan School of Management is the business school of the Massachusetts Institute of Technology, located in Cambridge, MA. MIT Sloan offers business education, including bachelor's, master's, and doctoral degrees. It also offers executive education in the form of an MBA program, one of the most selective in the world. Due to its emphasis on innovation and research, MIT's school of management has produced many influential business ideas and models.*

*In the following viewpoint, authors from the MIT School of Management argue that there has been a transformation to the workplace that involves the decentralization of management. The authors discuss ways in which both workers and organizations can benefit from this process, which has been inspired by evolving kinds of wisdom of the crowd-style collective intelligence and connectivity, which themselves have been spurred on by new technology. Some of the benefits possible with a more egalitarian management style include higher worker motivation, and increased creativity and enthusiasm, although the authors note that among not-so-wise crowds there may be potential risks.*

"Will Collective Intelligence Change the Way We Work?" MIT Sloan School of Management, April 3, 2016. Reprinted by permission

We're in the midst of a transformation in how businesses are organized. Typical corporate hierarchies are starting to look overrated, and changes in coordination technology have the power to make work and innovation even more democratic. However, according to MIT organizational theorist Thomas Malone, most of us are still victims of a centralized mindset, the idea that in order to manage things it's best to put somebody in charge who gives orders to other people. He urges us to look at the many new ways of organizing that allow more people to have more involvement in decisions—and for better results.

"Most people don't begin to realize how important and how pervasive and, in many cases, how desirable those new ways of organizing are going to be," said Malone, Professor of Management at MIT Sloan and the Founding Director of the MIT Center for Collective Intelligence, in a conversation with *MIT Sloan Management Review* Editor-in-Chief, Michael S. Hopkins. "At the Center, we are looking at how people and computers can be connected so that collectively they act more intelligently than any one person, group, or computer has acted before." When taken seriously, this question leads to a view of organizational effectiveness that is very different from the prevailing wisdom of the past.

## The New Paradox of Power: Give It to Gain It

The most rapidly evolving kinds of "collective intelligence"—a phenomenon where a shared or group intelligence emerges from the collaboration and/or competition of many individuals—are those enabled by the Internet. Wikipedia and YouTube are the best-known examples of collective intelligence. Similarly, InnoCentive is a web community that outsources companies' research problems and invites answers from anyone who wants to contribute, awarding a handful of cash prizes to the best of the bunch. And at MIT, the Climate CoLab uses crowdsourcing to harness the collective intelligence of thousands of people all over the world in an attempt to solve the problems of climate change.

## Will Collective Intelligence Change the Way We Work?

These design patterns presented in technology-enabled collective intelligence [are] also represented more generally in the shift from traditional hierarchies to flatter organizational structures. For years, pockets of the US military have been slowly taking decisions out of the hands of high-ranking commanders and entrusting them to teams of soldiers, who are told what problems to solve but not how to solve them. And last year, Zappos adopted a controversial flat organizational structure referred to as "holacracy." By order of CEO Tony Hsieh, the company abolished managers, eliminated job titles, denounced its organizational hierarchy and instead adopted a radical new system of self-governance. Automattic, the firm behind WordPress, only employs a couple hundred people, who all work remotely, with a highly autonomous flat management structure. GitHub is another highly successful firm with a similar structure.

Malone's book from 2004, *The Future of Work: How the New Order of Business Will Shape Your Organization, Your Management Style, and Your Life*, proposed that in an increasingly networked world, strict hierarchies would be less viable. The book also foreshadowed the decentralized "bottom-up" management model that has influenced companies like Zappos.

Another example of collective intelligence at its best is apparent in a different kind of workforce altogether—that of honeybees. As revealed by the research of Thomas Seeley at Cornell University, honeybees select the very best site at least 80% of the time—without the influence of the queen bee. By working together as a unified system, the organization (bee colony) is able to amplify its intelligence well beyond the capacity of any individual member of the group. And they do this with no bosses or workers—with no hierarchy at all.

Louis Rosenberg is CEO of Unanimous A.I., a "swarm intelligence company" that develops technologies for collective intelligence that allow groups to combine their thoughts and feelings in real-time, to answer questions, make decisions, or just have fun. Like Malone, he believes that if there are ways for companies to make smarter decisions, it's worth understanding them and exploring if new technologies can help us implement such methods.

Rosenberg authored an article on Next Web in which he references the honeybee phenomenon and its influence on "human swarming," a practice of connecting teams through specialized networking software that allow them to form closed-loop systems and tackle problems as a unified intelligence. One such platform modeled after biological swarms is called UNUM, which enables online groups to work in real-time synchrony, collaboratively exploring a decision-space and converging on preferred solutions in a matter of seconds. Real-world testing suggests it has great potential for harnessing collective intelligence.

"I often refer to what I call in my book the paradox of power," says Malone. "That's the idea that sometimes the best way to gain power is to give it away. Linus Torvalds, the developer of the Linux open source operating system, gave power away to thousands of programmers all over the world and was rewarded with a different kind of power. Pierre Omidyar, the founder of eBay, and the CEOs who followed him at that company, gave power away to their customers, and were rewarded with a different kind of power." Read more on *MIT Sloan Management Review* (https://sloanreview.mit.edu/article/a-billion-brains-are-better-than-one/)

## The Risks of Not-So-Wise Crowds: Boaty McBoatface

Even a relatively flat organization can have barriers to unleashing their collective intelligence, however. As Malone's research on group intelligence and the measurement of that intelligence shows, some groups are clearly smarter than others. This differentiation can be attributed to a variety of factors, including the degree to which all group members participate equally, social perceptiveness within the group, and the number of women in a group. To learn more about Malone's research, watch his INNOVATION@WORK webinar, Building Better

Organizations with Collective Intelligence (http://executive.mit.edu/media-video/mit-sloan-executive-education/building-better-organizations-with-collective-intelligence-webinar-with-tom-malone/hu4zxr40bsa).

Groups that are less effective include those that operate more like herds—a single individual darts in one direction and the rest of the group follows. This herding tendency is exacerbated by social media and other modern technologies that enable random impulses to go viral. For example, a study out of MIT, Hebrew University of Jerusalem, and NYU shows that if you randomly assign the first vote in an up-voting system like Reddit, that single first opinion will influence the final result by 25%, even if thousands of votes follow.

In other words, not all crowds are as wise as we'd like to think. The United Kingdom recently asked the public to help name its new, state-of-the-art polar research ship. As reported on NPR, the UK was seeking an "inspirational name" that exemplifies the "vessel's mission, a historical figure, movement, landmark, or a famous polar explorer or scientist." Alas, the current front-runner in the Internet-based poll, is "Boaty McBoatface." While this is amusing from a news perspective, it does demonstrate the potential risks faced when organizations try to leverage the "wisdom" of crowds. To be fair, the man who coined the front-running name was attempting to be funny and had no idea he'd inspire a such a herd effect.

## Where Collective Intelligence Makes Sense

In the shift toward the decentralized workplace, Malone says we're likely to see these changes first in the places where the benefits are most impactful. "The benefits of having lots of people make decentralized decisions are that people are more highly motivated, they work harder, they're often more creative," says Malone. "They're willing to be more inventive, to try out more things. They're able to be more flexible when they can adapt to the specific situation in which they find themselves rather than having to follow rigid rules sent down from on high that may or may not apply in this particular situation. And often, they just plain like it better."

Those benefits of decentralized decision-making won't be important everywhere. "In, say, certain kinds of semiconductor manufacturing, the biggest benefits come from things like economies of scale, and we may see more centralization to take advantage of that. But in a knowledge-based and innovation-driven economy, in high tech, R&D-oriented industries, the critical factors of business success are often precisely those benefits of decentralized decision making: freedom, flexibility, motivation, creativity."

According to Malone, in cases where a decentralized way of working actually works better, those new companies will have an advantage. They'll grow or be replicated by lots of other similar companies. And eventually, the old companies that haven't figured out how to change themselves will either be acquired or go out of business or belatedly imitate the new ways of doing things.

There is a growing body of evidence that shows that organizations with flat structures outperform those with more traditional hierarchies in most situations. There are other forces at work as well that may make it imperative to test out new, flatter organizational structures. Young employees and millennials, for example, don't respect hierarchy for the sake of itself. They want fast-moving, lean platforms on which to build their work. Technology is also lowering barriers to entry—small, capable teams are creating enormously valuable businesses with seed capital in software and hardware at a fraction of the cost of big company R&D. New experiments have never been easier or cheaper to conduct.

Ask yourself, what are the specific actions you might hope to do in new ways because of collective intelligence? Are you trying to create new products? Are you trying to make decisions faster? Who should be making these decisions? There are now many opportunities for decisions to be made by people not only

### Will Collective Intelligence Change the Way We Work?

throughout organizations, but outside of organizations, like customers and suppliers.

Of course, decentralization, communication technologies, and collective intelligence can't and won't take the place of leadership, or even make it less important. These new ways of working will just put more weight on leadership qualities like vision, encouragement, and inclusion.

# 11

## Witness to an Information Cascade: The Dangers of Herd Mentality

*Claire Potter*

*Claire Potter is a professor of history and the Executive Editor of* Public Seminar *at The New School in New York City. Her latest book, written with Renee Romano, is titled* Historians on Hamilton: How a Blockbuster Musical Is Re-staging America's Past *(Rutgers, 2018). Her research areas focus on recent political history in the United States, sexuality, gender and the media, and digital studies.*

*In an information cascade, instead of making independent decisions based on personal knowledge, expertise, or further researching the issue, people observe the choices of others in the crowd and follow their example. This herd-like behavior can lead to startingly wrong or inaccurate choices. The theory is used in the field of behavioral economics and other social sciences and the phenomenon is especially prevalent (and can be exploited) among users of social media. Claire Potter discusses her experience with the #CovingtonBoys social media fiasco of January 2019 in her public seminar selection here.*

Everyone has a #CovingtonBoys story, and this is mine. It is a story about clickbait. It is a story about how an unknown political operative captured a real event that might never have been noticed at all, and turned it into a news tsunami during

"How I Knew the #CovingtonBoys Video Was Clickbait | Public Seminar" by Claire Potter, medium.com, February 24, 2019. https://clairepotter.com/2019/01/24/how-i-knew-the-covingtonboys-video-was-clickbait-public-seminar/. Licensed under CC BY 4.0 International.

a federal government shutdown that has imperiled millions of Americans. And it is about why a powerful story about race in America makes it almost impossible to talk about how you got that story in the first place.

## The Tweet

I was on Twitter last Sunday evening when the one-minute video popped up, tweeted from an account I did not recognize. "This MAGA loser gleefully bothering a Native American protester at the Indigenous People's March," the four-minute video was captioned. In a tight shot, filmed by a steady hand, the white high school student we now know as Nick Sandmann stood, smiling. To the right, an older man, later identified as Omaha Nation elder and military veteran Nathan Phillips, chanted and beat a drum, inches away from Sandmann's face. In the background, other white boys, also in MAGA hats, aimed their phones at the pair, clapped, hollered, leaped around, and laughed.

I watched it through, aware of the retweet widget turning over rapidly. It was going viral.

Because I did not really understand what the video meant to the thousands sharing it, I clicked on the response widget on the far left to look at comments. I learned Sandmann and Phillips' names; that the group of white students were from Covington Catholic in Kentucky, and that they were in Washington for the March for Life. Phillips, I learned, a tribal elder, had been blocked by Sandmann as he tried to get to the Lincoln Memorial to complete a ritual for that day's Indigenous People's March (this version of the story soon changed).

The other students, I read, had begun to chant "build that wall," mocking Phillips with the "tomahawk chop" gesture still used by professional and college sports fans. I learned that the Black Hebrew Israelites (identified by the Southern Poverty Law Center as a black supremacist group whose confrontations with "perceived enemies are growing uglier and gaining increasing attention through video clips circulated to legions of viewers on websites like YouTube") had been harassing the group from Covington for over an hour.

I watched the video again, and was surprised to see and hear none of what I had just read, only aware that the students were Trump supporters because of their MAGA hats. I could not read the students' gear to confirm what school they attended, I heard no "build that wall" chant and saw no "tomahawk chop." There was no evidence as to how the two men had ended up facing each other. No one was carrying a sign for the March for Life, and the video was shot so tightly, there was no evidence that they were at the Lincoln Memorial.

*How did people know these things?* I thought. Answer: they didn't. At least, not from that first video.

Back in the comments, things had gotten worse. I saw a list of emails and phone numbers where I could voice my outrage about the students' disrespect for Phillips. I saw that the school's website had already crashed. On Facebook, I read that Sandmann was "smug," a "smirking bastard," who a lot of adult white men wanted to hurt. One wanted to "pulverize" him; another saw him as a boy he would "really enjoy punching in the face." A third fantasized about "taking a baseball bat to all of them."

I replied: "What kind of a person gets excited about punching and beating high school students?"

## Who Was @2020fight?

I searched the web and found that the school had already apologized for the incident (only to retract the apology later, when they came to believe that it was their own students who had been attacked.) Several longer videos, taken from different angles and in different time frames, showing that many more people had been involved, and that Phillips had approached Sandmann, while an unseen man near Phillips had yelled at the Covington students that they were on stolen land and should "go back to Europe." I went to the account that had tweeted the video, which was spammy, and then traced the tweet back to a second account, @2020fight, that was even spammier: a few hours later, CNN would report that @2020fight was a fake account, controlled in the US but appearing to emanate from Brazil, and that the video had been boosted by a network of 40 other fake accounts. Twitter suspended it. I consulted with some other journalism colleagues: we compared notes, and traded new videos. We all agreed that there was something deeply wrong with the story.

The next day, I did something I have never done before, which was to identify the video as professional clickbait on my own social media feeds, asking my networks not to repost it until they were fully informed. I warned them about the threats of violence and permanent harm to reputation that could be the outcome of a social media mob, and wrote that my research had shown that Phillips approached Sandmann, not the reverse. I wrote about the taunts aimed at the Covington students as Phillips approached. "A bunch of us spent time on this yesterday," I reported, "and our findings match the findings that are being published in conservative media. And none of us heard [the students] chanting `Build that wall.'"

But these elements of the story remained in place, even as new evidence appeared, and people continued to share.

## The Facts

The short answer is that there are facts, but so far they aren't lining up with each other, and they probably won't for some time until the lawyers start deposing people. But if you don't know what passed between the Black Hebrew Israelites, the students of Covington High School, and Nathan Phillips, here are some accounts I have found helpful and/or reliable.

- The map. The physical encounter between the parties compiled on Twitter was meticulously traced by veteran organizer Lisa Sharon Harper. Formerly of Sojourners and now the President of Freedom Road, Harper attended the Indigenous People's March subsequently watched multiple videos, and provides a map of how everyone moved around the space and what they did. Although it is a partisan account,

Harper did not hear "Build the Wall" either, and does not repeat the things that many have found difficult to verify.
- The timeline. Most news outlets began by posting unresearched, reactive accounts of the event based on social media reports that they have since retracted, and in some cases, apologized for. Tuesday's article in the *Washington Post* is a fairly accurate account of what we do and do not know.
- The Native American perspective. For a summary of the coverage and backgrounders on Nathan Phillips by *Indian Country Today*, the most prominent outlet for Native American national news, go here: https://newsmaven.io/indiancountrytoday/news/a-summary-of-indian-country-today-s-coverage-on-nathan-phillips-and-magayouth-BEjWHt1qb0eMO2shg6MYdQ/.
- Personal statements. One of Phillips' accounts of the event is here: https://reason.com/blog/2019/01/20/covington-catholic-nathan-phillips-video; Nick Sandmann's only statement, written in consultation with a public relations firm, is here: https://www.cnn.com/2019/01/20/us/covington-kentucky-student-statement/index.html.

## What #Covingtonboys Tells Us About Social Media

I think the most underreported story about #CovingtonBoys is how it got to us in the first place. It originated with a piece of clickbait that was chosen and edited, by persons unknown, to produce outrage on the right and the left. Originating in a fake account, and proliferated by other fake accounts, it was part of a professional social media campaign intended to disrupt. No one seems to know yet who filmed and edited the first, one-minute video, or who is behind the fake accounts: on Wednesday, the Democratic leadership of the House Intelligence Committee requested that Twitter provide details of their own investigation.

I hope we will have them sooner, rather than later. But what I was most surprised by was that, even when I began to provide confirmation that the story had its origins in a clickbait campaign, similar to those we experienced in the 2016 election, the vast majority of people in my network (who were themselves disparaging the Covington students to a greater or lesser degree, and some viciously) dismissed this actual evidence completely.

It surprised me that people who had been so sure that the presidency had been stolen from Hillary Clinton by Facebook and Cambridge Analytica completely dismissed the possibility that their feeds had been hacked again. At its worst, friends and acquaintances often characterized my views as deluded, disappointing, and a distraction from the urgency of what was clearly, to them, an emergent racial justice crisis. In one case, an interlocutor told me flat out that I was lying, without a glance at the link to the CNN investigation that I had provided. Many expressed dismay that, if I pursued the clickbait story, I would contribute to the misapprehension that the Covington students were "innocent" (something I had never said, since I think it is an inappropriate way of describing anyone who is not Jesus, or a newborn baby). Some believed that my intent was to deliberately undermine and discredit Phillips, which was also not my goal.

I want to stipulate that I care deeply about racism, and racial violence. I understood friends' and colleagues' concern that their distress about the encounter at the Lincoln Memorial might be invalidated by changing the subject to why and how it had come to their attention in the first place. Because of this, as I was having these conversations on social media, I decided to temporarily abandon my current reading to prioritize work by feminists of color, to make sure I always had critical voices in my head. I read Brittney Cooper's *Eloquent Rage*, a pleasure I had put off for too long; dipped back into Audre Lorde's Sister Outsider, and re-read favorite essays from J. Kehaulani. Kauanui and Robert Warrior's recent collection, *Speaking of Indigenous Politics*.

I recommend this as a strategy, because it is an antidote to how stupid and ruminative we all become on social media. It helped me listen to others better. It helped me to detect when I needed to express my love and respect for an interlocutor, and it helped me remember to always express appreciation for the knowledge that they brought to our dialogue.

But social media has its own logic, and this is why clickbait works: people filter online information through their deepest belief systems. As we know from the 2016 election, challenging someone's read of clickbait is tantamount to challenging their most cherished principles, and such exchanges need to be suspended and move off line before friendships are damaged. Thus, I did not succeed in persuading anyone who did not already believe it that the campaign of online violence against the Covington students and their families was disproportionate to the actual harm that had occurred at the Lincoln Memorial, or that the professional clickbait campaign was an urgent story, unless they were already open to that perspective. One white male correspondent even scoffed at the idea that anyone should fear death threats "because they are never real."

Spoken like someone who has never received a death threat, right? Most importantly, even when I could persuade people that they were responding to a professional clickbait campaign, one that had managed to target an impressive range of the political spectrum from left to right, I could not persuade them to really privilege the knowledge. When I asked people whether they thought they might have been targeted for the video because of data they left behind during the Kavanaugh hearings and the 2016 campaign, they scoffed at the idea.

## Clickbait Is at Least as Dangerous as Fake News

So, what's the takeaway—for now?

First, as a nation, despite all the hearings about Facebook and angsty rage about our data privacy, the vast majority of intelligent users have learned very little about how social media works and why their own behaviors are complicit in the success of clickbait campaigns. Most people also still confuse clickbait with fake news. But the most effective clickbait is rarely fake; it is a real event that has been provoked, manipulated, decontextualized, and algorithmically boosted. Clickbait is designed to incite a highly emotional response that will cause the viewer to share. (Think Hillary's "basket of deplorables." Or the Hulk Hogan sex tape.) Currently there is another clickbait video from a Twitter account called @roflinds, in which a young woman asserts that "The Covington Catholic boys harassed my friends and I before the incident with Nathan Phillips even happened. I'm tired of reading things saying they were provoked by anyone else other than their own egos and ignorance." Nothing in the video identifies even the faces of the harassing boys: as of Tuesday, it had been watched 50,000 times, and picked up by a clickbait site called indy100 and by The Root, a news and opinion site that publishes from a critical race perspective. People are sharing the video, not because the video itself identifies the boys as being from Covington, but because white boys who are racists are misogynists too—right? In other words, they mistake it for evidence that supports their view of the #CovingtonBoys, when a slightly closer look demonstrates that it does not.

Second, people usually do not track an internet item back to the source to verify it: when I asked different individuals how they got some of the Covington material they posted, including the original video, they said: "a friend." But when pressed as to which friend, it turned out that it wasn't anyone they knew, and they had no idea what the point of origin was. Ironically, one piece people sent me in response to my concerns was Laura Wagner's "Don't Doubt What You Saw With Your Own Eyes," an essay for the anti-Covington set to reassure them that snap judgements, based on everything you already know, are the best judgements, and that information does not need to be vetted.

But no one seemed to notice that this article was published at Deadspin, part of the Gizmodo empire, a media conglomerate that has always specialized in shifty clickbait news that hurts people for the sake of advertising click-throughs. To learn more about this, read Ryan Holiday's *Conspiracy*.

As importantly, look at the tight shot of Sandmann and Phillips together: to a racial justice advocate, Sandmann looks like a self-confident bully. But imagine yourself as a person who believes white boys are under attack by the left: in this scenario, Sandmann looks like a restrained and heroic youth holding his own in a tough situation. That's what good clickbait does: it works because it reinforces what you already know. The phrase "MAGA loser" in the original tweet was genius in that regard. It perfectly activated anti-Trump partisans who do, in fact, believe that MAGA hat-wearing people are losers; and Trump supporters who know that they are regarded that way and resent it deeply. It's why fake tweets, like the one purportedly from Nick Sandmann's mother advocating Native American genocide, are persuasive: we already "know" her son is a racist. Now we know why!

Third, ask yourself: do academics and activists actually believe that people instinctively know the truth when they see it? Is this what we teach in our classrooms? Is this not a major critique of the criminal justice system—that white people make snap, and lethal, judgements about people of color because of the biases that they bring to encounters? Do we not recall how outraged we were when selectively edited videos led to Congressional hearings about Planned Parenthood selling fetal tissue illegally? Are we not fully aware that people are framed every day because they have been misidentified in a line-up; or killed because someone "felt" they were dangerous? For more about how this relates to a broad-based belief that Nick Sandmann was showing racist contempt for Nathan Phillips, see Molly Callahan's "You Think You Can Read the Facial Expression on the Teenager in the MAGA Hat? You Can't."

Finally, do we really believe, as a country, in destroying lives over the internet? I do not know how the vast factories of clickbait sites will be contained; or if mainstream news organizations can bring themselves to pull back from relying on uncorroborated social media feeds themselves. But part of what we need to be honest about is how much people love to identify an enemy and attack them; how cathartic social media mobs are; and how righteous they make us feel. The disproportionate and permanent costs to real people, and to our political culture, are profound, but in the moment, we don't really care.

Currently, people are mocking the well-to-do Sandmann family for hiring a tony PR firm, but anyone in social media knows they would be stupid not to do it, because it is the only way to get out from under a Twitter mob. I will be interested in the coming days if anyone can make a solid argument for how this episode advanced racial justice, or even racial awareness. But what I do know is that it did not bring us any closer to being ready for the social media attacks that will accompany the 2020 election.

# 12

# 10 Things You Ought to Know About Polls
## Bill Schneider

*Bill Schneider is an American journalist who served as CNN's senior political analyst from 2000–2009. He is currently the Omer L. and Nancy Hirst Professor at George Mason University's School of Public Policy. In 2009, the International Foundation for Electoral Systems presented Schneider with a special award "for his extensive coverage and keen insight of the 2008 United States presidential elections … showcasing democracy in action."*

*In the following viewpoint, Bill Schneider, who is familiar with the ins and outs of reporting on polls during the American political election cycle, relates how poll taking is more of a complex art form than anything that should be taken as concrete black and white truth. He shows how this method, utilizing the wisdom of crowds, can be a helpful tool to gain understanding and perspective, but that the process is fallible and that polls reflect opinion and are not indicative or predicative of behavior.*

Some of us love polls and some of us hate polls. Most of us love them and hate them at the same time.

We love them when they tell us something we like to hear—such as the fact that nearly 90 percent of Americans favor background checks for gun purchasers.

---

"10 Things You Ought to Know About Polls," by Bill Schneider, The Communications Network. Reprinted by permission.

We hate them when they get things wrong—like in this year's midterm election when polls kept telling us that many Senate races would be close. They weren't.

Here are ten things you ought to know about polls.

## 1. Polls Are Not Designed to Be Predictive

You've heard this before: polls are a snapshot of the way people feel at that particular moment. Things can change. They often do.

All the polls this year showed Republicans leading Democrats going into the midterm. They just didn't show how big a lead Republicans would eventually have. It's likely that most of the people who told polltakers they "didn't know" or were "not sure" how they were going to vote ended up voting Republican. 2014 was the "Nobama election," and late deciders (who are typically very weak partisans) got swept up in the mood of the country.

## 2. Randomness Is the Key to Polling

How can a sample of one thousand respondents represent the views of 245 million voting-age Americans? The answer is, you have to follow elaborate procedures to make sure that every adult American has a mathematically equal chance of being interviewed. If respondents are truly picked at random, their responses can be inferred to the whole adult population within an acceptable margin of error (often plus or minus 5 percent).

Random selection is not easy. Or cheap. A lot of younger people are rarely at home. And they don't have land lines. The public is increasingly wary of callers who may be trying to sell them something. Or asking for a contribution. Nowadays, it takes as many as 20 attempts before you can complete an interview with someone willing to spend 15 minutes on the telephone.

Pollsters now try to reach some people on their cell phones. That can be expensive. Batteries give out. Pollsters are also interviewing people over the Internet. But many lower income people don't have Internet access. So pollsters try to weight their samples to compensate for people who are hard to reach.

Some pollsters are even giving up on true random samples. Instead they are using panels of respondents purposely selected to represent the adult population—imposing quotas for, say, Republicans and unmarried women and retirees. That's risky and controversial. If you select the known percentage of, say, men under 30, you may be ignoring other factors like education or race.

The hardest thing to do is to identify "likely voters." Ask people if they intend to vote in the coming election and 80 percent will say "Yes." Yet fewer than 40 percent actually voted this year. Pollsters try to identify likely voters by asking people whether they voted in the last election, whether they know where their polling place is, how closely they are following the campaign, etc. Then they lop off the 40 percent who seem most likely to vote and call them "likely voters." That's not science. It's educated guesswork.

## 3. It's Often Difficult to Tell a Good Poll from a Bad Poll

You have to be cautious. If the responses seem out of line, check the make-up of the sample. Are there too many Democrats? Not enough African-Americans? Too many seniors? And check the wording of the questions. That can make a huge difference (see #6 below).

Generally speaking, reputation matters. Polls that regularly release their findings to the public—with information about survey procedures and question wordings—are usually pretty good. That includes most polls done for the media (the *CBS News–Washington Post* poll, the *NBC News–Wall Street Journal* poll, the *ABC News–Washington Post* poll, etc.). It also includes non-partisan polls that regularly release their findings to the press (Pew Research Center, Gallup). Those polls live and die by their reputations, so they have to be more careful.

## 4. No Single Poll Should Ever Be Taken as Authoritative

No, not even polls taken by academic institutions (like the University of Michigan Survey Research Center, the National Opinion Research Center at the University of Chicago, the Quinnipiac University poll, the Marist College poll). Those polls are usually pretty reliable. But they are not immune from differences caused by different question wordings and "noise" (unavoidable random variation).

The best way to look at polls is to look at several of them taken at about the same time asking similar questions. If they all show roughly the same thing—like a Republican trend in 2014—you can feel more confident that the result is true. If the polls are all over the place, beware. But even gold standard polls like Pew and Gallup should never be taken as authoritative.

## 5. Polls of Specific Subgroups Can Be Tricky

Suppose you want a sample of African-Americans. Interviewing people who live in heavily black neighborhoods may be the cheapest way to find respondents. But you will be excluding a lot of African-Americans who live in mixed neighborhoods. They may have very different views.

Suppose you want a sample of Jews. It's not a good idea to go out looking for Jews, by interviewing people in kosher markets or people with religious insignia on their doorposts. You may end up with a sample of very religious Jews, whose views are often quite different from those of more secular Jews. Some pollsters interview people with "distinctive Jewish names" (Cohen, Goldberg, etc.). But they would miss people like Daniel Radcliffe, the actor who played Harry Potter and who happens to be Jewish (who knew?).

The best way to sample subgroups is to let them fall into your larger sample at random. If you interview 1,000 Americans, about 25 of them will likely identify themselves as Jewish. That's not a large enough sample for statistical reliability. But if you combine Jewish respondents who fell into twenty different national samples at random, you will end up with 500 Jews. That's about the minimum size for a reliable sample.

## 6. Words Matter

Always look at the way poll questions are worded. That can make a huge difference. Ask people their opinion of the Affordable Care Act and you will get one answer. Ask them their opinion of "Obamacare" and the answer is likely to be different.

A 2013 Gallup poll press release was headlined, "In US, Most Reject Considering Race in College Admissions." The question asked whether college applicants should be admitted solely on the basis of merit, "even if that results in few minority students being admitted," or should applicants' racial and ethnic backgrounds be considered to help promote diversity, "even if that means admitting some minority students who otherwise would not be admitted." Answer: stick to merit, 67 to 28 percent.

Now here's the headline of a Pew Research Center press release from 2014: "Public Strongly Backs Affirmative Action Programs on Campus." The Pew question asked, "Do you think affirmative action programs designed to increase the number of black and minority students on college campuses are a good thing or a bad thing?" By better than two to one (63 to 30 percent), the Pew respondents said affirmative action is a good thing. The public supports programs that help disadvantaged groups meet the prevailing standards of competition. The public opposes making exceptions to those standards for certain groups.

Or take the case of immigration. "Amnesty" for illegal immigrants is not very popular. But the public supports allowing people who came to the US illegally to obtain legal residence if they meet certain conditions (pay a fine, have an otherwise clean record, speak English, have a job, pay taxes). It all depends on how you ask the question.

Another example: a Yale University poll found "Americans Much More Worried about `Global Warming' than `Climate Change.'" Global warming sounds dangerous. Climate change sounds natural.

## 7. Beware of Complex Questions

Why? Because if you give respondents many different signals, you don't know which ones they are actually responding to.

Here's a question from a poll taken this summer:

*Now I am going to read you some things a Republican is saying about the economy and what needs to be done to make things better. Please tell me whether you find it very convincing, somewhat convincing, a little convincing or a not at all convincing statement about the economy and how to make it better.*

*President Obama has failed on the economy. The middle class is struggling with declining paychecks, high unemployment and the rising costs of health care, college and even a tank of gas. Bigger government, higher spending and never-ending deficits are not the answer. We need to repeal Obamacare, cut regulations and lower taxes. We need to build the Keystone pipeline and use our energy to create jobs and lower gas prices. We can bring back opportunity and balance the budget and spark an economic recovery if we get big government out of the way.*

As it happens, 72 percent of likely voters found that statement "somewhat" or "very" convincing. But what exactly did they find convincing? That President Obama has failed on the economy? That we should repeal Obamacare? Cut taxes? Build the Keystone pipeline? Balance the budget? There's no way to tell because all those signals are bundled together.

## 8. Respondents Tend to Think a Poll Is a Quiz

Have you ever listened to a poll interview over the telephone? I have. Many times. Here's what often happens.

The interviewer asks, "Do you favor or oppose sending US ground troops to help people in Ukraine resist Russian aggression?"

The respondent thinks about it—often for the first time—and answers the question cautiously, "No, I don't think that would be a good idea ... Um, was that the right answer?"

Questions should never give any clue that the question has a right answer. Because respondents are inclined to impress the interviewer. That's also the reason why telephone polls often work better than in-person interviews. Over the telephone, people feel less compelled to try to impress the interviewer.

Some polls do away with human interviewers altogether. They "robocall" respondents and ask them to answer questions by pushing buttons on their phones ("Press 1 if your answer is yes and 2 for no"). Robocalls have many problems, but no one feels compelled to impress a machine (unless they think someone is secretly recording their answers).

## 9. Polls Are Opinions, Not Behavior

People sometimes express opinions that may or may not reveal what they would actually do. Gallup asks people if they would vote for a generally well-qualified candidate for President who happens to be a woman. In 2012, 95 percent said yes. That may be because they know what the right answer is: "Of course I would vote for a woman. I'm not prejudiced."

But would they? What the poll may actually reveal is that people know what the social norms are: don't endorse prejudice. In the same poll, 68 percent said they would vote for a gay or lesbian candidate for President. 58 percent said they would vote for a Muslim candidate. But are they saying that because they think those are the right answers?

## 10. A 50-50 Result Does Not Necessarily Mean People Are Sharply Divided

Ask people whether they would prefer to have apple pie or ice cream. The answer you get would be something like 50 percent pie and 50 percent ice cream. Is that because the public is deeply polarized between pie-lovers and ice cream-lovers? No. It's because people like both. They are picking a response at random.

Polls have asked Americans whether they consider Edward Snowden a hero or a traitor. The results usually come out to about 50–50. A lot of people can't make up their minds about Snowden, or feel that he is both. The 50–50 result seems to suggest that Americans are deeply divided over Snowden. What it may reveal is that people are picking an answer at random. That's what happens if you force people to make a choice when they feel both ways, or don't have a strong opinion. They shrug.

# 13

## Introducing the Global Brain: How Ideas Will Spread in 2035

*Michael Haupt*

Michael Haupt is a writer and speaker based in Cape Town, South Africa. He is an advocate for what he calls whole system transcendence and is the author of a forthcoming book, Society 4.0—The Epic Story of the Game that Birthed a Civilisation.

*In the following futuristic viewpoint, Michael Haupt introduces us to the emerging concept of the Global Brain, a collective knowledge system that will allow everyone to access and contribute knowledge equally, without the influence of middlemen and other powerful people. Haupt claims that what we currently know as cloud technology will very soon evolve into a repository of all the world's knowledge, available for access at any time by anyone, truly a wisdom for the crowds.*

There are two major differences between knowledge in your world and knowledge in our world:

- The primary knowledge focus in your world is on people, events and scores; our primary focus is on ideas.
- Knowledge in your world flows through a series of influencers; in our world we are able to tap directly into the source of knowledge.

"Introducing the Global Brain: How Ideas Spread in 2035," by Michael Haupt, Medium.com, June 30, 2017. Reprinted by permission.

# Introducing the Global Brain: How Ideas Will Spread in 2035

Throughout the history of Western civilisation, all inventions came about because of a desire to reduce the friction involved in moving ideas around and moving physical goods around. Papyrus letters and ink, the printing press, ships, airplanes, trains, newspapers, satellites, TV and radio, telephones, telegrams, mobile phones and the Internet were each new inventions that progressively reduced the friction involved in moving things around. The process of sharing news a hundred years ago with someone on the other side of the world took at least 2 weeks. You had to write a letter, which would be delivered across the ocean via ship and finally taken to the recipient's door on horseback. Nowadays you can share news with anyone on the planet instantaneously.

With each new leap forward, the method by which news was shared became cheaper, faster and smaller. Today you can share news from the palm of your hand using a smartphone with more computing power than all of NASA had in 1969. In our world, progress has allowed us to remove the technological device completely and we simply tap into the Global Brain directly. We are able to communicate with anyone instantly and we can access any knowledge immediately. You are learning how to do this by using filesharing applications and a concept you call The Cloud. The Cloud is slowly evolving and will soon become The Global Brain—a repository of all the world's knowledge, accessible by anyone, anywhere.

In your world you are required to interact with technology by typing. A few devices are able to recognise your voice, but many of them are unreliable and the interaction often proves frustrating. In our world, our thoughts connect directly to technology and there is no delay between our request and a response.

Making sense of life in your world is somewhat challenging because you are constantly bombarded with a maelstrom of inconsequential and irrelevant facts and figures: random news events from around the globe, weather and traffic reports, financial analyses, social media updates from people you follow and political talking heads repeating ill-conceived opinions ad nauseam.

Micro-snippets of information are the order of the day. One of the characteristics of left brain thinking is to examine each idea or news event as an isolated incident, and so seeing patterns in your world requires a lot of effort.

It's a common fallacy in your world that everyone only uses 10% of their brain. The reality is that you're only able to access 10% of the world's knowledge. Even the most well-educated and intelligent people in your world know very little. That's because of how the spread of ideas is affected in your world by two factors:

- Influencers (also known as middlemen), and
- The principle of Style over Substance.

In your world it's assumed that the best ideas—the one's that are most logical and useful—are the ideas that win. It's commonly accepted that your national, cultural or religious history evolved because of a process of the best ideas bubbling to the surface. However, even sociologists accept that there's questionable evidence for this assumption. In short, ideas in your world are spread by people with influence, and what is best for people with influence isn't always what's best for everyone else.

In addition, the people who have the best ideas often don't possess the skills of being influential. As you've seen in your own politics, a charismatic senator or presidential candidate often has far worse ideas than their brilliant, but awkward, rival. In your world, the spread of an idea depends on the social power of the initiator.

You see the same thing happening in business in your world, where a product no one needs is marketed so well that it overcomes a healthier, cheaper alternative that fails to excite or compel customers to buy.

When it comes to evaluating ideas in your world, the effects of influencers and style over substance have kept many of your world's best ideas hidden, and this is significantly slowing your progress. The good news is that you will break through fake news, filter bubbles and cognitive bias as soon as The Global Brain is launched.

The Global Brain maps all of the world's ideas and shows their connection to other ideas. Anyone can submit ideas quickly and easily and ideas can be sorted by topic, recency, impact and evolutionary progress potential. The visual map is interactive and anyone can navigate and explore to any depth they'd like. There are no influencers in the process of spreading ideas and each person's Daily Briefing introduces them to new ideas relevant to their level of wisdom. The Global Brain helps us spread ideas and advances our society quickly.

## Summary

Your knowledge systems are built and designed for the transmission of facts and figures about people and events. Knowledge in this format has served a left brain dominated society effectively for hundreds of years, but as we developed our right brains, we needed a knowledge system that spread ideas. The Global Brain was our solution.

# 14

## Better Wisdom from Crowds
### Peter Dizikes

*Peter Dizikes writes about social sciences, business, and humanities at the MIT University News Office. He has also reported and written articles on intellectual life, science, and politics for* The New York Times, The Boston Globe, The Washington Post, Salon, *and* Slate, *among others. He attended Columbia University and New York University.*

*The following viewpoint explains the significance of "surprisingly popular," a method for improving the accuracy of the wisdom of crowds phenomenon developed by two scholars at MIT along with an associate at Princeton University. This new algorithm suggests that those participants in a crowd who know their choices will not be popular should, in essence, be given more attention. Researchers found that this new algorithm reduced prediction errors by more than 20 percent.*

The wisdom of crowds is not always perfect. But two scholars at MIT's Sloan Neuroeconomics Lab, along with a colleague at Princeton University, have found a way to make it better.

Their method, explained in a newly published paper, uses a technique the researchers call the "surprisingly popular" algorithm to better extract correct answers from large groups of people. As such, it could refine wisdom-of-crowds surveys, which are

"Better Wisdom from Crowds," by Peter Dizikes, Massachusetts Institute of Technology, January 25, 2017. Reprinted with permission (http://news.mit.edu/).

used in political and economic forecasting, as well as many other collective activities, from pricing artworks to grading scientific research proposals.

The new method is simple. For a given question, people are asked two things: What they think the right answer is, and what they think popular opinion will be. The variation between the two aggregate responses indicates the correct answer.

"In situations where there is enough information in the crowd to determine the correct answer to a question, that answer will be the one [that] most outperforms expectations," says paper co-author Drazen Prelec, a professor at the MIT Sloan School of Management as well as the Department of Economics and the Department of Brain and Cognitive Sciences.

The paper is built on both theoretical and empirical work. The researchers first derived their result mathematically, then assessed how it works in practice, through surveys spanning a range of subjects, including US state capitols, general knowledge, medical diagnoses by dermatologists, and art auction estimates.

Across all these areas, the researchers found that the "surprisingly popular" algorithm reduced errors by 21.3 percent compared to simple majority votes, and by 24.2 percent compared to basic confidence-weighted votes (where people express how confident they are in their answers). And it reduced errors by 22.2 percent compared to another kind of confidence-weighted votes, those taking the answers with the highest average confidence levels.

The paper, "A Solution to the Single-Question Crowd Wisdom Problem," is being published today in *Nature*. The authors are Prelec; John McCoy, a doctoral student in the MIT Department of Brain and Cognitive Sciences; and H. Sebastian Seung, a professor of neuroscience and computer science at Princeton University and a former MIT faculty member. Prelec and McCoy are also researchers in the MIT Neuroeconomics Laboratory, where Prelec is the principal investigator.

## A Capital Idea

To see how the algorithm works in practice, consider a case the researchers tested. A group of people were asked a yes-or-no question: Is Philadelphia the capital of Pennsylvania? They were also asked to predict the prevalence of "yes" votes.

Philadelphia is not the capital of Pennsylvania; the correct answer is Harrisburg. But most people believe Philadelphia is the capital because it is a "large, historically significant city." Moreover, the people who mistakenly thought Philadelphia is the state capital largely thought other people would answer the same way. So they predicted that a very high percentage of people would answer "yes."

Meanwhile, a certain number of respondents knew that Harrisburg is the correct answer. However, a large portion of those people also anticipated that many other people would incorrectly think the capital is Philadelphia. So the people who themselves answered "no" still expected a very high percentage of "yes" answers.

That means the answer to the two questions—Is Philadelphia the capital? Will other people think so?—diverged. Almost everyone expected other people to answer "yes." But the actual percentage of people who answered "yes" was significantly lower. For this reason, the "no" answer was the "surprisingly popular" one, since it deviated from expectations of what the answer would be.

And since the "surprisingly popular" answer differed in the "no" direction, that tells us the correct answer: No, Philadelphia is not the capital.

The same principle applies no matter which direction responses deviate from expectations. When people were asked if Columbia is the capital of South Carolina, the opposite happened: More people answered "yes," compared to their expectations of how many people would say "yes." So the surprisingly popular answer was, correctly: Yes, Columbia is the capital.

## The Wisdom of Subsets of Crowds

In this sense, the "surprisingly popular" principle is not simply derived from the wisdom of crowds. Instead, it uses the knowledge of a well-informed subgroup of people within the larger crowd as a diagnostically powerful tool that points to the right answer.

"A lot of crowd wisdom weights people equally," McCoy explains. "But some people have more specialized knowledge." And those people—if they have both correct information and a correct sense of public perception—make a big difference.

This is the case across scenarios that the researchers tested. Consider art. The researchers asked art professionals to guess the price range for different contemporary artworks. Individually, art experts selected price ranges that were typically too low, perhaps because selecting a lower range is a reasonable, safe answer for an artwork that the expert does not recognize. Collectively, this makes the majority opinion of an expert panel even more biased in the direction of low prices.

And this is where the "surprisingly popular" principle makes a difference, since it does not depend on an absolute majority of expert opinion. Instead, suppose a relatively small number of experts believe a piece sold for $100,000, while anticipating that most other people will think it sold for less. In that case, the evaluations of those experts will lead the "surprisingly popular" answer to be that the artwork was more expensive than most people thought.

"The argument in this paper, in a very rough sense, is that people who expect to be in the minority deserve some extra attention," Prelec says.

## Recovering Truth

The scholars recognize that the "surprisingly popular" algorithm is not theoretically foolproof in practice. It is at least conceivable that people could anticipate a "surprisingly popular" opinion and try to subvert it, although that would be very hard to execute. It is also the case, as they write in the *Nature* paper, that "These claims are theoretical and do not guarantee success in practice, as actual respondents will fall short of ideal."

Other scholars who have studied collective-wisdom problems believe the method is valuable. Aurelien Baillon, a professor of economics at Erasmus University in Rotterdam, who has read the paper, calls it an "exciting" result that "opens up completely new ways to think about an old problem." Baillon finds the paper persuasive, he adds, because it contains both theoretical arguments "and empirical evidence that it works well."

Baillon does note that the question of how people reach conclusions about the beliefs of others "can still be further explored" theoretically. And he observes one potential practical pitfall in the method: the possibility that all participants in a survey do not have useful knowledge about what others think and make a random choice if given two options. Such a 50/50 split, Baillon observes, means the "surprisingly popular" answer would simply be the majority result.

Still, the researchers themselves hope their work will be tested in a variety of settings. In the paper they express confidence that the "surprisingly popular" principle will prove durable, asserting: "Such knowledge can be exploited to recover truth even when traditional voting methods fail."

# 15

## When the Wisdom of Crowds Fails
### Nick Beim

*Nick Beim is a venture investor and technology enthusiast who attended Oxford University and currently lives in New York City. His writing and interests focus primarily on artificial intelligence, big data, software, and fintech investments. He blogs on the economics of innovation at www.nickbeim.com.*

*In the following viewpoint, author Nick Beim suggests that the core principal of the wisdom of crowds failed in the United Kingdom's recent Brexit decision. His argument is not for elitism, nor does he feel all democratic decisions must result necessarily in poor results defined by mob rule, but instead believes that the wisdom of the crowd is best served when the crowd is truly informed by a free press and that decision makers are educated about their choices and the parameters of their choices.*

I do not believe in the collective wisdom of individual ignorance." —Thomas Carlyle, Scottish philosopher and historian.

Crowds can be remarkably unwise, particularly on complex subjects where the stakes are highest.

There is no charitable way to discern wisdom in the result of the Brexit vote. This isn't a judgment about political values or how the British economic pie is divided. It's an observation about the dramatic reduction in pie for the whole country—not just

"When the Wisdom of Crowds Fails" by Nick Beim, Medium.com, June 29, 2016. Reprinted by permission.

economically, but in the UK's influence in the world, its national unity, its national security and its innovative capacity.

Many Brits who voted for the leave campaign appear to be waking up to this fact as the British pound has plummeted to its lowest level in 30 years against the US dollar, British stockmarkets have been hammered, Nigel Farage disavowed a core promise of the Leave campaign hours after victory, and congratulations have poured in from Putin, Le Pen and other foreign unsavories.

British voting centers have been inundated with calls from people wishing they could change their vote, and there is petition with over 3 million signatures for a do-over referendum. Google reported a big spike in British searches for "what is the EU" the day after the referendum, and counties heavily reliant on EU subsidies, which disproportionately voted in favor of a Brexit, have suddenly realized they are in financial trouble and are desperately seeking assistance.

This could have happened anywhere. If the US Constitution were put to a referendum in 1787 instead of being debated by delegates, it would almost certainly have been defeated. The proposal was a radical one that was unpopular at the time in many quarters, and the popular vote would have been easy prey for the agrarian populists and Tammany Hall politicians who opposed it.

Instead it was crafted, debated, endlessly modified and barely pushed through by a group of delegates that were not even themselves elected but chosen by state legislatures. Given that the US became the world's longest-lived constitutional democracy and most prosperous economy, it is hard in retrospect to argue with the wisdom of that particular group.

Which is not to argue for elitism but to say that the wisdom of crowds works when the crowd is informed. Bottoms-up economic decision-making of individuals, families and firms tends to lead to optimal pricing and the most efficient allocations of capital and labor. Individuals voting for political candidates when there is a free press and active debates tends to be effective in taking the balanced measure of these candidates. Open source software evolves through distributed expertise and community review.

But holding a referendum on something as complex as EU membership when most citizens couldn't reasonably be expected to fully understand how it would affect them is a more challenging proposition. Experts are needed, even for other experts. Deliberation and debate are needed. Explanation is needed. Then more deliberation and debate are needed.

But on complex issues where strong emotions are involved, that's not what a referendum invites, and that's not what happened in the UK. Fear-mongering and misinformation, amplified by social media and a sensationalist press, created what one young Brit despairingly called "a post-factual democracy." The primary motivation of the Leave campaign appeared to be registering anger and protest rather than make a well-reasoned decision.

The wisdom of crowds is rightly one of the core principles underlying modern democracy, economics and innovation. But it doesn't work if the crowds aren't informed, if the decisions are too complex for any person to fully understand or if voters' emotions can be heavily manipulated. And it's often on the most important questions—like membership in a political union or the creation of a constitution—where these things are true.

Representative democracy, for all its flaws, tends to work better on the big questions than direct democracy. Representative democracy forces deliberation into the mix, a political virtue that is arguably growing in importance as the world becomes more complex and as social media threatens to narrow the political mind to instant reactions and quick fixes. In liberal democracies, it also dissipates anti-minority sentiments, which appear to have played a significant role in the Brexit vote.

It's a thought worth considering as technology will increasingly enable more direct democratic participation, a trend that for the most part is profoundly empowering. Electronic voting, when it eventually arrives in the US, will bring far more people into political decision-making and can lead to a more politically informed and engaged electorate. Direct democracy and referenda can be valuable tools for making narrow political decisions where the impact of those decisions is clear, but they tend to limit deliberation and increase the likelihood of the manipulation of voters in the most complex and emotionally charged decisions, which can sometimes mean making the wrong choices where it counts most.

# 16

## Groupthink Can Lead to Bad Decisions and Hinder Innovation

### Phil McKinney

*Phil McKinney is former Chief Technology Officer at Hewlett-Packard. He is author of* Beyond the Obvious, *host of the Killer Innovations podcast, and president and CEO of CableLabs.*

*Groupthink, a term coined in 1972 by a social psychologist, is the tendency of individuals to surround themselves with people very similar to themselves. This sameness can lead to poor judgment and decisions, and perhaps worse, it can hinder innovation and entrepreneurship. The following viewpoint provides several examples of groupthink and ideas for avoiding it.*

Research on small groups has found that people in groups tend to "like" people who are most like them. They tend to establish norms or limits to behavior to make sure similarity and harmony is nurtured or even enforced. This normal group behavior can turn into a problem, however, because breakaway ideas that may cause fractures in the group norms are necessary for the group to progress and innovate.

The term "groupthink" was coined by social psychologist Irving Janis in 1972. It happens when behavioral norms are enforced to

---

"If You Want to Innovate then Avoid the Herd. Groupthink Leads to Bad Decisions," by Phil McKinney, February 25, 2016. Copyright of Phil McKinney and The Innovators Network. Reprinted by permission.

maintain group cohesiveness but lead to "a deterioration of mental efficiency, reality testing and moral judgement."

## Symptoms of Groupthink

Janis documents eight symptoms of groupthink, as quoted by Psychologists for Social Responsibility:

1. Illusion of invulnerability—Creates excessive optimism that encourages taking extreme risks.
2. Collective rationalization—Members discount warnings and do not reconsider their assumptions.
3. Belief in inherent morality—Members believe in the rightness of their cause and therefore ignore the ethical or moral consequences of their decisions.
4. Stereotyped views of out-groups—Negative views of "enemy" make effective responses to conflict seem unnecessary.
5. Direct pressure on dissenters—Members are under pressure not to express arguments against any of the group's views.
6. Self-censorship—Doubts and deviations from the perceived group consensus are not expressed.
7. Illusion of unanimity—The majority view and judgments are assumed to be unanimous.
8. Self-appointed "mindguards"—Members protect the group and the leader from information that is problematic or contradictory to the group's cohesiveness, view, and/or decisions

## Bad Decisions

Groupthink leads to bad decisions because it encourages members of the group to ignore possible problems with the group's decisions and discount the opinions of outsiders. When members of the group are too comfortable with each other, similar in background, or become insulated from outside influences and information, groupthink can be a big problem. It influences decisions most when there are no clear rules for decision making.

Groupthink is especially dangerous in business groups where cohesiveness is backed up by financial rewards and personal advancement, along with the threat of exclusion. Often, as executive coach Dr. Pete Stebbins notes, groups make internal value judgments that are unfair to those outside the group. When that happens, though, there are no or few consequences because there's little accountability to anyone outside the group.

Teams that have developed a strong in-group familiarity from long association may feel comfortable making decisions in isolation, believing their decisions will never be challenged. Notable examples of this occur all the time in the banking and financial industries—if you've seen the recent Oscar-nominated film *The Big Short*, you'll see what I mean.

Essentially, in a group that has succumbed to groupthink, any viewpoints that may contradict the general consensus of the group are self-censored to preserve cohesiveness. Groupthink symptoms include a collective sense of invulnerability and overconfidence, when members rationalize away problems and explain away threats to success. Members begin to consider membership as a mark of superiority, and justify their actions as part of a greater good that only they can see. And they disregard new ideas that may call their past assumptions into question.

## Examples of Groupthink

In July 2001, Swissair, the Swiss national carrier, which had been so financially stable that people called it "the flying bank," suddenly collapsed. Just before that, Swissair insiders eliminated much of the industrial and technical expertise from its governing board. This decision is regarded by many as the result of insider groupthink, reducing dissonance that threatened cohesiveness on the board.

In 1999, the members of the Major League Umpires Association were so convinced of their unified position that 54 of them resigned en masse, thinking they could force negotiations with MLB for a new labor agreement. Groupthink robbed them of their ability to consider the likely outcome. The baseball owners accepted and finalized the resignations of 22 umpires, hiring new ones. MLB de-certified the union, which was eventually replaced by the World Umpires Association.

## Combating Groupthink

Combating groupthink has been the subject of a lot of research since Janis introduced the idea in 1972. While it can be insidious and hard to change once it's taken root, groupthink can be fought—it just takes concrete strategies that ensure dissenting opinions are heard.

### Formalize the Questioning Process

Groups should organize regular feedback reviews where each member is expected to come up with a reservation or problem regarding the project or problem being worked on. These discussions can really get members to question the group's decisions. The fact that the objections are mandated by the group rules removes the threat of disapproval by other members.

### Institute Anonymity

There should always be a way for group members to anonymously raise concerns about ideas or solutions the group comes up with. Many people, regardless of group cohesiveness, feel uncomfortable bringing up objections in a group, especially when they're less experienced or newer members. There could be a document where group members can contribute questions and concerns anonymously, or a designated team member with whom others should bring these up.

### Bring in Outsiders

Chances are, you won't have an in-group expert on every aspect of a project. Bringing in outside specialists to investigate the group's ideas can ensure that nothing is overlooked or ignored if it doesn't fit neatly into the group's vision.

## *Allow Extra Time*

Often, tight deadlines can exacerbate the problems of groupthink because it's easier to just "get it done" in the easiest way than to really take a close look at the work. Extra time should always be built into projects for decisions to be examined and reconsidered before anything is permanent.

## Conclusion

Groupthink is a risk when any number of people works together closely for an extended period of time. That kind of group cohesiveness can produce amazing results, but it can also lead to bad decisions because the group's assumptions aren't regularly questioned. Just as individual innovators have to constantly question the status quo in the world at large in order to come up with truly new ideas, this same process has to play out in groups of innovators, who should always question their own group's conclusions.

# Organizations to Contact

*The editors have compiled the following list of organizations concerned with the issues debated in this book. The descriptions are derived from materials provided by the organizations. All have publications or information available for interested readers. The list was compiled on the date of publication of the present volume; the information provided here may change. Be aware that many organizations take several weeks or longer to respond to inquiries, so allow as much time as possible.*

**American Psychological Association**
750 First St., NE
Washington, DC  20002-4242
(800) 374-2721
website: www.apa.org

The American Psychological Association is the leading scientific and professional organization representing psychology in the United States, with more than 118,000 researchers, educators, clinicians, consultants, and students as its members. The organization's mission is to promote the advancement, communication, and application of psychological science and knowledge to benefit society and improve lives.

**Crowdsourcing Week**
7 Henrietta St.
Covent Garden
London WC2E 8PS
United Kingdom
(347) 586-9862
email: hello@crowdsourcingweek.com
website: www.crowdsourcingweek.com

Crowdsourcing Week is an organization that provides information and ideas to individuals and groups on crowdsourcing and crowd innovation. It holds conferences, programs, and workshops on these topics across the globe.

**The Global Brain Institute**
CLEA
Vrije Universiteit Brussel
Pleinlaan 2, B-1050 Brussels, Belgium
+32-2-640 67 37
email: info@globalbraininstitute.org
website: www.globalbraininstitute.org

The Global Brain Institute was created in 2012 in Brussels, Belgium. It issues scientific statements designed to help understand the connectivity between humankind, networks and machines.

**GoFundMe**
855 Jefferson Ave.
P.O. Box 1329
Redwood City, CA 94063
website: www.gofundme.com

GoFundMe is broadly considered the leader of the available free online fundraising/crowdfunding sites, operating since 2010. Since its inception, it has helped to raise more than $5 billion in over 170 countries.

**Intellipedia**
website: https://www.intelink.gov/my.logout.
php3?errorcode=19

Established in 2005, Intellipedia is a Wikipedia style intelligence and data sharing system established online and used by the U.S. intelligence community. The networks are not open to the public, but some documents can be accessed through the Freedom of Information Act (FOIA).

## International Open Source Network (IOSN)
National Telehealth Center
University of the Philippines Manila
Taft Avenue, Manila
Philippines 1000
+63 2 525 6501
email: info@iosn.net
website: https://web.archive.org/web/20060804090521/http://iosn.net/

IOSN, also known as FLOSS (Free and Open-Source Software), is an organization that states its slogan is "software freedom for all." It advocates free technology solutions to developing nations and other countries around the world.

## Lumenogic
475 Longview Rd.
South Orange, NJ 07079
(917) 502-2831
website: www.lumenogic.com

Formerly known as News Futures, Lumenogic is a prediction market company that utilizes collective intelligence to forecast information relative to business, sports, politics and other diverse fields. It harnesses some of the best aspects of the wisdom of the crowds concept to produce accurate results without groupthink.

## Simplicable
website: www.simplicable.com

Simplicable is described as a technology and business guide that explains modern ideas in a simple, nonbiased way. Definitions and information on information cascades and other elements of social media and tech networks can be found on their site.

## Organizations to Contact

### Sloan Neuroeconomics Lab
MIT E94-1561
245 First St.
Cambridge, MA 02142
(617) 258-9889
email: chollan@mit.edu
website: www.nel.mit.edu

The Sloan Neuroeconomics Lab is a research center housed by the Massachusetts Institute of Technology and dedicated to the study of economic theory and decision analysis. The scholars there are responsible for the creation of "Surprisingly Popular," an algorithm designed to perfect the wisdom of crowds.

### Social Media Today
575 Eye St. NW, 4th Floor
Washington, DC 20005
(202) 331-2480
email: info@industrydive.com
website: www.socialmediatoday.com

Social Media Today provides networking and original analysis on social media and the social media industry. It features an industry focused publication operated by Industry Dive, a company that produces business-related journalism.

### StopBullying.gov
US Department of Health and Human Services
200 Independence Ave. SW
Washington, DC 20201

StopBullying.gov is a federal government website managed by the US Department of Health and Human Services. StopBullying.gov provides information from various government agencies on what bullying is, what cyberbullying is, who is at risk, and how you can prevent and respond to bullying. StopBullying.gov coordinates closely with the Federal Partners in Bullying Prevention Steering Committee, an interagency effort co-led by the Department of Education and the Department of Health and Human Services that works to coordinate policy, research, and communications on bullying topics.

**Wikipedia**
Wikimedia Foundation, Inc.
1 Montgomery St., Suite 1600
San Francisco, CA 94104
(415) 839-6885
email: info@wikimedia.org
website: www.wikipedia.org/

Described on its landing page as "the free encyclopedia that anyone can edit," Wikipedia is hosted by the Wikimedia Foundation, a nonprofit organization that sponsors other open source projects. These include Wikiuniversity, free learning materials and activities, and Wikivoyage, free travel guides, among many other open source materials.

# Bibliography

## Books

Gina Arnold, *Half a Million Strong: Crowds and Power from Woodstock to Coachella*. Iowa City, IA: University of Iowa Press, 2018.

Daren C. Brabham, *Crowdsourcing*. London, UK: The MIT Press, 2013.

Mark Hedges and Stuart Dunn, *Academic Crowdsourcing in the Humanities: Crowds, Communities and Co-Production*. Cambridge, MA: Elsevier, 2018.

Kim R. Holmes, *The Closing of the Liberal Mind: How Groupthink and Intolerance Define the Left*. New York: Encounter Books, 2017.

Jefferey C. Hood, *Inefficient Market Theory: An Investment Framework Based on the Foolishness of the Crowd*. Seattle, WA: Amazon Digital Services, 2014.

Helene Landemore, *Collective Wisdom: Principles and Mechanisms*. New York: Cambridge University Press, 2012.

Thomas W. Malone and Michael S. Bernstein, *Handbook of Collective Intelligence*. Cambridge, MA: MIT Press, 2015.

Lisa Lynn Miller, *The Myth of Mob Rule: Violent Crime and Democratic Politics*. New York: Oxford University Press, 2018.

Mar W. Moffett, *The Human Swarm: How Our Societies Arise, Thrive, and Fall*. London, UK: Head of Zeus, 2019.

Jeremy Rifkin, *The Zero Marginal Cost Society: The Internet of Things, the Collaborative Commons, and the Eclipse of Capitalism*. New York: Palgrave Macmillan, 2015.

Kiruba Shankar and Mitchell Levy, *#Crowdsourcing Tweet Book01: 140 Bite-sized Ideas to Leverage the Wisdom of the Crowd*. Cupertino, CA: THiNKaha, 2011.

Nikki Springer, *James Surowiecki's The Wisdom of Crowds: Why the Many Are Smarter than the Few*. London, UK: Routledge, 2018.

Robert J. Sternberg and Jennifer Jordan, *The Cambridge Handbook of Wisdom*. New York: Cambridge University Press, 2018.

Cass R. Sunstein and Reid Hastie, *Wiser: Getting Beyond Groupthink to Make Groups Smarter*. Boston, MA: Harvard Business School Press, 2015.

James Surowiecki, *The Wisdom of Crowds: Why the Many Are Smarter than the Few*. London, UK: Abacus, 2014.

Nathaniel Tkacz, *Wikipedia and the Politics of Openness*. Chicago, IL: University of Chicago Press, 2015.

Christopher L. Tucci, Allan Afuah, and Gianluigi Viscusi, *Creating and Capturing Value Through Crowdsourcing*. Oxford, UK: Oxford University Press, 2018.

Alan Watkins, Iman Stratenus, and Ken Wilber, *Crowdocracy: The End of Politics*. Chatham UK: Urbane Publications, 2016.

## Periodicals and Internet Sources

Daniel Akst, "The Wisdom of Even Wiser Crowds," *The Wall Street Journal*, February 16, 2017. https://www.wsj.com/articles/the-wisdom-of-even-wiser-crowds-1487265722.

Phillip Ball, "The Wisdom of the Crowd: The Myths and Realities," bbc.com, July 8, 2014. http://www.bbc.com/future/story/20140708-when-crowd-wisdom-goes-wrong.

# Bibliography

Mark Buchanan, "Want Wisdom? Be Your Own Crowd," *Bloomberg*, January 17, 2018. https://www.bloomberg.com/opinion/articles/2018-01-17/want-to-get-wisdom-be-your-own-crowd.

D. Cassino, "The 'Wisdom of the Crowd' Has a Pretty Bad Track Record at Predicting Jobs Reports," *Harvard Business Review*, July 8, 2016. https://hbr.org/2016/07/the-wisdom-of-the-crowd-has-a-pretty-bad-track-record-at-predicting-jobs-reports.

Emily Dreyfus, "A Wild Plan to Crowdsource the Fight Against Misinformation," *Wired*, April 17, 2019. https://www.wired.com/story/claire-wardle-ted-2019-crowdsource-against-misinformation/.

Amanda Hess, "Some Online 'Mobs' Are Viscious. Others Are Perfectly Rational," *New York Times Magazine*, August 7, 2018. https://www.nytimes.com/2018/08/07/magazine/some-online-mobs-are-vicious-others-are-perfectly-rational.html.

Brandon Keim, "Sharing Information Corrupts Wisdom of Crowds," *Wired*, May 16, 2011. https://www.wired.com/2011/05/wisdom-of-crowds-decline/.

Graham Kendall, "How to Unleash the Wisdom of Crowds," The Conversation, February 9, 2016. https://theconversation.com/how-to-unleash-the-wisdom-of-crowds-52774.

Olga Khazan, "The Stupidity of the Crowd," *Bloomberg*, July 29, 2013. https://www.bloomberg.com/opinion/articles/2018-01-17/want-to-get-wisdom-be-your-own-crowd.

Maria Konnikova, "The Wisdom of Crowds, Revisited: When the Crowd Goes from Wise to Wrong," Bigthink, May 31,

2011. https://bigthink.com/artful-choice/the-wisdom-of-crowds-revisited-when-the-crowd-goes-from-wise-to-wrong.

Emilie Le Beau Lucchesi, "What Turns Black Friday Shoppers into Raging Hordes?," *New York Times*, November 21, 2017. https://www.nytimes.com/2017/11/21/well/mind/the-psychology-of-the-black-friday-shopping-mob.html.

Eric Luellen, "On the Wisdom of Crowds: Collective Predictive Analytics," *Towards Data Science*, May 2, 2017. https://towardsdatascience.com/on-the-wisdom-of-crowds-collective-predictive-analytics-302b7ca1c513.

Scott McLemee, "'The Wisdom of Crowds': Problem Solving Is a Team Sport," *New York Times*, May 22, 2004. https://www.nytimes.com/2004/05/22/books/review/the-wisdom-of-crowds-problem-solving-is-a-team-sport.html.

George Musser, "Metaknowledge: Crowds Aren't as Smart as We Thought, Since Some People Know More than Others. A Simple Trick Can Find the Ones You Want," Aeon.com, July 6, 2016. https://aeon.co/essays/a-mathematical-bs-detector-can-boost-the-wisdom-of-crowds.

Jeffrey Rosen, "America Is Living James Madison's Nightmare," *The Atlantic*, October 2018. https://www.theatlantic.com/magazine/archive/2018/10/james-madison-mob-rule/568351/.

Erin Ross, "How to Find the Right Answer When the 'Wisdom of the Crowd' Fails," *Nature*, January 24, 2017. https://www.nature.com/news/how-to-find-the-right-answer-when-the-wisdom-of-the-crowd-fails-1.21370.

Lee Siegel, "Go the Same Way, or Go the Wrong Way," *New York Times*, May 3, 2013. https://www.nytimes.com/2013/05/05/fashion/seeking-out-peer-pressure.html?pagewanted=all&_r=0.

# Bibliography

Dana G. Smith, "The Wisdom of Crowds Requires the Political Left and Right to Work Together," *Scientific American*, March 8, 2019. https://www.scientificamerican.com/article/the-wisdom-of-crowds-requires-the-political-left-and-right-to-work-together/.

Leighton Vaughan Williams, "How the Wisdom of Crowds Could Solve the Mystery of Shakespeare's 'Lost Plays,'" The Conversation, April 14, 2016. https://theconversation.com/how-the-wisdom-of-crowds-could-solve-the-mystery-of-shakespeares-lost-plays-57705.

"What Psychology Experiements Tell You about Why People Deny Facts," *Economist*, December 8, 2018. https://www.economist.com/united-states/2018/12/08/what-psychology-experiments-tell-you-about-why-people-deny-facts.

"Wisdom of the Crowd Accurately Predicts Supreme Court Decisions," *Technology Review*, December 26, 2017. https://www.technologyreview.com/s/609852/wisdom-of-the-crowd-accurately-predicts-supreme-court-decisions/.

# Index

## A
Affordable Care Act/Obamacare, 92, 93
Africa, 61
African Americans, 90, 91
Allport, Floyd Henry, 20
Aristotle, 7
artificial intelligence (AI), 62, 67, 68
Automattic, 73

## B
Baillon, Aurelien, 104
Ball, Philip, 14
Beim, Nick, 105
Bellamy, Edward, 31
Berger, Victor L., 32
Bian, Lin, 43–48
Black Hebrew Israelites, 79, 81
Blair, Tony, 18
Boaty McBoatface, 74, 75
Brexit, 39, 105, 106
Brown, Justine, 58
Burke, Edmund, 36

## C
California State University, 68
Callahan, Molly, 86
Cambridge Analytica, 83
censorship, 25, 26, 110, 111
Challenge.gov, 58

*Challenger*, 12–13
Cimpian, Andrei, 43–48
clickbait, 78, 81, 84–86
climate change, 61, 72, 92–93
Climate CoLab, 72
Clinton, Hillary, 83, 85
Cloud technology, 96, 97
CNN, 81, 82, 83
collective intelligence, 37, 38, 39, 62–69, 71–77
Communism, 31, 33–34
#Covingtonboys, 78, 82, 85
Craven, John, 13
crowd collaboration, 58, 59
crowdfunding, 10
crowd labor, 58, 60
crowdsourcing, 9, 13, 35, 37, 52, 56–61, 62, 72
crowd voting, 58, 59

## D
Deadspin, 85
Debs, Eugene V., 32–33
democracy, 7, 9, 19, 28–34, 35, 59, 60, 61, 106–108
Democratic socialists, 30, 31–32
Democrats, 46, 48, 82, 89, 90
dissociation, 24–26
diversity, 9, 11, 14, 15, 17, 19, 92
Dizikes, Peter, 100

# Index

## E
eBay, 74
economic inequality, 30, 34
Ellis, Joseph, 29
Estonia, 59
European Union (EU), 39, 106, 107

## F
Facebook, 59, 80, 83, 84
fake news, 84, 98
Farage, Nigel, 106
Federalist Papers, 29
Feynman, Richard, 13
Finland, 59–60
Founding Fathers, 9, 28, 29, 30
Freud, Sigmund, 8, 25

## G
Gallup poll, 28, 34, 90, 91, 92, 94
Galton, Francis, 11, 12, 17
German Pirate Party, 60
Global Brain, 9, 96–99
Google, 106
Great Depression, 33
group fallacy, 23, 24, 26
group mind, 20, 22, 23
groupthink, 109–113

## H
Hamilton, Alexander, 29–30
Harper, Lisa Sharon, 81–82
Haupt, Michael, 96
Hayek, Friedrich A., 33, 36, 38, 54
Health Datapalooza, 58
herd mentality, 78
Hokkaido University (Japan), 65
honeybees, 73–74
Hopkins, Michael S., 72
Hsieh, Tony, 73
human swarming, 9, 62–69, 74
Hutton, Will, 15

## I
Iceland, 59
immigration, 39, 92
Indigenous People's March, 79, 81
influencers, 96, 98, 99
InnoCentive, 72
Internet, 7, 9, 18, 52, 55, 56, 72, 75, 85, 86, 89, 97
Isidore of Seville, St., 53, 55

## J
Janis, Irving, 109, 110, 112
Jews, 91–92
Johnson, Lyndon B., 30, 34
Jussim, Lee, 40, 41, 42, 43, 46, 47, 48, 49

## K
Kendall, Graham, 11
Keynes, John Maynard, 18
Khatib, Talal Al-, 28

Koerth-Baker, Maggie, 56–57, 59, 60

## L

Le Bon, Gustave, 8, 22
Leslie, Sarah-Jane, 44
Library of Congress, 59
Linux, 74
Liquid Feedback, 60
*Looking Backward* (Bellamy), 31

## M

Mackay, Charles, 36
Madison, James, 29
Major League Umpires Association, 112
Malaysia Airlines Flight MH370, 13
Malone, Thomas, 72–76
Marx, Karl, 31
Massachusetts Institute of Technology (MIT), 71, 72, 75, 100, 101
McCarthy, Joseph, 33
McCoy, John, 101, 103
McKinney, Phil, 109
mental conflict, 24, 25, 26–27
MIT School of Management, 71
mob rule, 7, 8–10, 28, 29, 105
morals, 15, 22, 48, 67, 110
Morton Thiokol, 12–13
Muslims, 44–45, 94

## N

National Aeronautics and Space Administration (NASA), 58, 97
Native Americans, 79, 82, 86

## O

Obama, Barack, 89, 92, 93
Omidyar, Pierre, 74

## P

Park, Todd, 58
Pew Research Center, 90, 91, 92
Phillips, Nathan, 79–83, 85–86
Planned Parenthood, 86
Plato, 21
polls, 7, 12, 28, 34, 37, 64–65, 67, 75, 88, 91–95
Polybius, 7
Potter, Claire, 78
Prelec, Drazen, 101, 103
press, 9, 18, 19, 90, 105, 106, 107
psychoanalysis, 24, 26
Psychologists for Social Responsibility, 110

## R

race, 79, 90, 92
racism, 83, 85, 86
Reddit, 75
Red Scare, 33
Reicher, Steve, 8

Republicans, 46, 48, 89, 90, 91, 93
Rivers, W. H. R., 24–26
*Road to Serfdom* (Hayek), 33
robocalls, 94
Roosevelt, Franklin D., 30, 33, 34
Rosenberg, Louis, 62, 73, 74

## S
Saddam Hussein, 18
Sanders, Bernie, 30
Sandman, Nick, 79–82, 86–87
Schneider, Bill, 88
*Scorpion*, 13
Seeley, Thomas, 73
Seung, H. Sebastian, 101
Simon, Julie, 35
Snowden, Edward, 95
social conflict, 20, 24, 26
socialism, 28, 30–31, 33, 34
social media, 59, 69, 75, 78, 81–84, 86, 87, 97, 107
social mind theory, 21, 22, 24, 25, 26
social psychology, 8, 20, 21, 22, 40–44, 48–49, 109
Southern Poverty Law Center, 79
Stebbins, Pete, 111
stereotypes, 40–49, 110
Surowiecki, James, 9, 12, 16–18, 37
Surprisingly Popular (algorithm), 9, 100–104

Swissair, 111
synchrony, 62, 63, 64, 65, 66, 68

## T
Tarde, Gabriel, 8
Thomas, Norman, 33
Torvalds, Linus, 74
Trump, Donald, 80, 86
trust, 40
Tucker, Jeffrey A., 52
@2020fight, 80–81
Twitter, 59, 79, 81, 82, 85, 87

## U
Unanimous AI, 62, 64, 66, 73
United Kingdom, 60, 75, 105
United States, 8, 9, 28–34, 60, 73, 92, 93, 106, 107
  elections, 28, 30, 32, 83, 84, 87, 88, 89, 90
University of Southern California, Los Angeles (UCLA), 68
UNU, 65, 67, 68, 69
US Constitution, 28, 29, 106

## V
Verhulst, Stefaan, 56
Von Hippel, Eric, 37
voting, 36, 37, 39, 65, 75, 89, 104, 106, 107

## W
Wagner, Laura, 85
Wales, Jimmy, 54–55

Warne, Shane, 16
Washington, George, 30
*Who Wants to Be a Millionaire*, 12, 17
Wikipedia, 9, 52–54, 57, 60, 72
*Wisdom of Crowds* (Surowiecki), 9, 11, 16, 17, 18, 37
wisdom of crowds phenomenon, 11, 100
World War I, 32
World War II, 33

# Y

YouTube, 72, 80

# Z

Zappos, 73